Reviewing Care Management
for Older People

Reviewing Care Management for Older People

Edited by Judith Phillips and Bridget Penhale

Jessica Kingsley Publishers
London and Bristol, Pennsylvania
and The British Society of Gerontology

First published in the United Kingdom in 1996 by
Jessica Kingsley Publishers Ltd
116 Pentonville Road
London N1 9JB, England
and
1900 Frost Road, Suite 101
Bristol, PA 19007, U S A
in association with The British Association of Gerontology

Copyright © 1996 the contributors and the publisher

Library of Congress Cataloging in Publication Data
Reviewing Care Management for Older People/edited by Judith Phillips and Bridget Penhale.
p. cm.
Includes bibliographical references and index
ISBN 1 85302 317 5 (pbk. : alk. paper)
1. Senile dementia–Patients–Care–Planning.
I. Phillips Judith (Judith E.) II. Penhale, Bridget, 1955-
RC524.E94   1995
362.1'9897683–dc20
95–32046 CIP

British Library Cataloguing in Publication Data
Reviewing Care Management for Older People
1. Social work with the aged – Great Britain 2. Dementia – Great Britain 3. Aged – Care – Great Britain
I. Phillips, Judith, 1959 - II. Penhale, Bridget III. British Society of Gerontology
362.6'0941

ISBN 1 85302 317 5

Printed and Bound in Great Britain by
Cromwell Press, Melksham, Wiltshire.

Contents

List of Figures xii
List of Tables xii

Preface ix
Judith Phillips and Bridget Penhale

1. Reviewing The Literature On Care Management 1
Judith Phillips

2. New Concepts, Old Responses: Assessment And Care Management Pilot Projects In Scotland 14
Alison Petch

3. Multi-Disciplinary Assessment and Care Management 28
Kerry Caldock

4. Needs-Led Assessment: The Practitioner's Perspective 40
Christine Futter and Bridget Penhale

5. On the Margins: Care Management and Dementia 60
Rosemary Bland

6. User Choice, Care Management and People with Dementia 71
Mary Winner

7. Research, Theory and Practice: Misunderstanding Verbal Language During Community Care Assessments 79
David Barrett

8. The Effects of Care Management on Efficiency in Long-term Care: A New Evaluation Model Applied to British and American Data 87
Bleddyn Davies, Barry Baines and John Chesterman

9. 'You wouldn't be interested in my life, I've done nothing': Care Planning and Life History Work with Frail Older Women   102

John Adams, Joanna Bornat, Mary Prickett

10. Ethnicity and Care Management   117

Elaine Cameron, Frances Badger and Helen Evers

11. Developing Care Management   134

Judith Phillips and Bridget Penhale

The Contributors   141

Subject Index   143

Author Index   146

List of Figures

2.1   Cupar – referral pathway   17

8.1   Case management inputs, other costs of community-based social and
community health care and average duration of stay in the community   89

8.2   Nursing home admission and case-load size for channelling sites   94

8.3   COCA case management costs and other home care costs in Sheppey
by four-week period   97

8.4   Cost relationships and care management parameters: setting parameters
to achieve an equitable and efficient balance of care   98

List of Tables

2.1   Pilot projects   15

2.2   Cupar – main needs   19

2.3   Duns – recording of needs   20

2.4   Duns – first prioritized needs identified according to discipline   20

2.5   Duns – needs and care plans   21

2.6   Duns – identification of needs by assessors   22

2.7   Alva – indicators of and for care management – care managed cases   25

2.8   Alva – indicators of and for care management – non care managed cases   26

5.1   Ages and Lutz scores of users with and without dementia and comparators   62

5.2   Gilleard problem checklist scores for problem frequency and seriousness
at first and second interview   65

5.3   Measured carer stress at first and second interview   67

8.1   Logit prediction of probabilities of transition from the community
to nursing homes   93

8.2   Rates of change in case management and other home care costs during
the COCA period in Sheppey   97

Preface

Judith Phillips and Bridget Penhale

There are a number of reasons for the appearance of this book. The original idea was to continue with the established tradition of publication following the British Society of Gerontology's annual conference. In this instance, the concept of a book on Care Management evolved from the 1993 annual conference, held in Norwich, which provided a number of papers reviewing the early arrangements and implementations of care management. Several other chapters were subsequently commissioned for the book concerning specific topics such as ethnicity and care management; multi-disciplinary assessment and care management; the practitioner's perspective on needs-led assessment.

The aims of this collection are to review the developments and implementation of several models of care management; to draw together research highlighting the success and difficulties in translating the principles of care management into practice, particularly in relation to empowerment, needs-led assessment and multi-disciplinary work; to assess the extent to which care management with its emphasis on user choice and participation can successfully be applied to older people suffering dementia and their carers; to examine ways of evaluating care management and finally to identify key areas for further development and research. We hope that the volume succeeds in these aims for the readership.

Chapter 1, by Judith Phillips, reviews the literature on care management from three specific angles. These are: an examination of the early publications on the topic (many of which developed from the work of the Personal Social Services Research Unit at the University of Kent). These were mainly academic texts focusing on the economic argument for care management. The second wave of publications to be examined are those produced and promoted by the Department of Health concerning the implementation of community care and care management arrangements and which provide advice and guidance for local authority social services staff. The final angle taken is to consider those publications which have been more critical of the concept of care management and which have developed a focus on the difficulties in applying theory to practice.

Following this introduction, Chapter 2, by Alison Petch, focuses on an evaluation of four of the pilot projects which were mounted by local authorities in Scotland in the run up to the implementation of the new community care arrangements. Evaluation was based on a number of dimensions, including multi-disciplinary assessment of needs, the selection of cases for care management and the perspectives of both assessors and service users on the process of assessment and care management. Two of the pilots provided services solely for elderly people; they were the major service users in the other two. This chapter, drawing across the projects, focuses on the extent to which the desired shift towards needs-led assessment was being achieved in practice, on the nature of the needs that were being identified and on the range of responses that were being offered. It seeks to locate the more detailed findings against the background of some of the major concepts outlined in the legislation and to highlight areas where practice and policy appear divergent.

The success of the community care reforms appears to be largely contingent upon the efficacy of multi-disciplinary working and assessment practices and this is addressed by Kerry Caldock in Chapter 3. Progress towards effectively functioning care management systems is unlikely to be achieved until multi-disciplinary assessment and co-operative working styles become well established. However, the frequent government exhortations to agencies and professions to 'work together' take little account of the historical and cultural differences that underpin the practice of separate agencies and professions. This chapter examines some of the differences in the ways assessment is conceptualized; paying particular attention to the long-establish dissension between social and medical models of assessment and care. The likely impacts of such differences on multi-disciplinary assessment and care management are explored and potential solutions considered.

Chapter 4, by Christine Futter and Bridget Penhale, focuses on the development of needs-led assessment with older people from the practitioner's perspective. The principal method employed is to take the perspective of the social work practitioner and to consider what the changes have meant for their practice, including consideration of case material where appropriate. Five main themes which can be identified from the overview of the literature are discussed: individualized assessments; choice; objective analysis of need; targeting and partnership with service users and their carers. From these themes, both theory and research are linked to case examples. The extent to which needs-led assessment is achievable in practice is examined. By way of conclusion, the contradictions which are apparent within both common understandings and expectations of the principles of needs-led assessment are summarized. The rhetoric of choice and independence is shown to to severely compromised by the realities which arise due to both rationing and priority setting which local authorities are having to undertake. Attention is also given to the lack of concordance between the emphasis on user involvement and managerialist tendencies which are apparent within and which at times appear to dominate the assessment process.

Chapters 5 (Rosemary Bland) and 6 (Mary Winner) address the issue of care management with dementia sufferers. A study of a pilot care management project in Scotland showed the project's success in alleviating the stress of carers of elderly people. However, where the elderly person had dementia, despite general subjective satisfaction with the support provided by care management, the measured morale of these carers did not improve over time. This raises the question of the morality of sustaining severely mentally impaired people at home when carer stress cannot be alleviated even by such intensive service provision. The rationale for care management has been that with careful targeting of those most at risk of institutionalization, it is possible to support frail elderly people at home cost-effectively. This chapter discusses the project findings in respect of people with dementia, identifies the dilemmas for care managers and asks whether such a service rationale, in terms of cost, should be applied to this group.

Mary Winner also raises the question whether the new rhetoric of community care and care management, with its emphasis on consumerism, user involvement and user choice, fits the needs and reality of people with dementia. Articulation of needs, wishes and consideration of alternatives would appear to be a prerequisite for this kind of involvement and decision-making. An alternative view that might be suggested is to use an advocate to perform this role – i.e. a person 'to talk on behalf of another'. But, how would such a person necessarily know the other person's wishes and preferences – especially if they have no previous knowledge or relationship with them? Much of the current literature on people with dementia focuses on the needs of the carer. It is sometimes suggested that carers could also be advocates, but this sometimes involves a conflict of interest on emotional, financial or practical levels. Does this approach necessarily involve empowering the person cared for?

If we cannot communicate reliably with people with severe dementia, how do we ensure that we are offering appropriate services to maximize the quality of life? Perhaps we should begin to start earlier – before the person requires complex care arrangements; when cognitive functioning is still sufficiently intact to express lifestyle preferences, priorities, preferred arrangements. Also, we need to begin to understand the individual person's biography as they relate it to us first hand. Living wills can be the formal arrangements. Care planning for people with dementia could beneficially start at an early stage of the illness and these early insights could be used to inform later work and decisions. It might also facilitate understanding of later behaviour. In order for this to occur, close liaison is necessarily required between health and social services. Further research would need to identify who the principal first point of contact was for people with dementia. This might well be the general practitioner (GP) in many, if not most, instances.

Chapter 7, by David Barrett, explores in depth the language used in assessment interviews illustrating the complexities in the process of assessment. Verbal language has been used in several different ways. What is expressed explicitly may not be the same as what is implied. Therefore different levels of meaning exist. This chapter argues that some parts of verbal language are used as a defence and a coping mechanism in a way that obscures the everyday realities of the low level of existence in which older people often live. It forms the basis of a rationalization, a good reason, but not the real reason, for self-description and can repress or ignore the unpleasantness of a day to day existence. This notion of using language as a coping and/or defence mechansism, when transferred to the arena of community care assessment, takes a very worrying turn because what is being said may not be what is meant. Coded messages may be given throughout an assessment interview. In conclusion, it is argued here that 'coded messages' could be a trigger in their own right for workers to look beyond presenting problems during assessment.

Bleddyn Davies, Barry Baines and John Chesterman in Chapter 8 review the effects of care management on efficiency in long-term care. The most common criterion applied in the evaluation of American programmes for long-term case management for elderly persons has been 'budget neutrality'. The relevance of the criterion has been increasingly questioned in the United States. There have been analyses of major data sets which imply other criteria, though each has had limitations. The chapter discusses criteria so far used, implied and proposed. It suggests that previous analyses have, perhaps, not directly tested the main effect on which the argument for care management depends: the effect on the costs of other services required to produce beneficial outcomes. It presents a new set of evaluative criteria based on direct and indirect consequences of the care management inputs in model form. It applies the new set of criteria in the analysis of the long-term care channelling data set and, more fully, the British Sheppey Community Care programme – an application of the model development in the Kent (Thanet) Community Care Project, the progenitor of the model of care management incorporated in British community care reform embodied in legislation of 1990 using logistic regression, regression, and 2SLS modelling. Results suggest some direct and indirect effects of the kind predicted by the theoretical model.

Joanna Bornat and her colleagues explore in Chapter 9 the use of life-history material in assessing need and planning care of frail older women in a continuing care setting. The literature on care planning is reviewed and evidence from recent research on the use of biographical information in producing a holistic appreciation of patients' needs is assessed. The chapter raises issues, drawn from particular interviews, around identity, empowerment and gender in relation to the setting of long term care.

Chapter 10 considers ethnicity and care management from the perspective of a series of interviews conducted during a research project. This study, commissioned by social services and the health authority, focused on the views, stories and experiences of old people and their carers and families as well as the perspectives of service providers.

Community care involves a commitment to the development of user-centred, needs-led and equitable services. Indeed, local authorities are obliged to consult with all sections of the community and to give users and carers a central role in decisions about their own care plans. However, these obligations often prove difficult for services to achieve in practice and all too often the reasons are given as inadequate funds and resources. This chapter argues that the reality is far more complex. Many service providers are unaware of the many ways in which they are failing to meet their commitments to some groups of people in the community, such as ethnic minorities. Resource levels are important but are only part of the picture. Proper consideration of ethnicity, along with other social factors such as class, gender, age and disability, is central to efforts to achieve the goals of community care. The research indicates that services can make significant progress towards meeting some of the goals of community care for disadvantaged groups.

By way of conclusion, in the final chapter Judith Phillips and Bridget Penhale draw together the main strands of the evaluations and analyses presented in this book. They outline the areas of care management that require further research and discussion and outline the principal issues for practice and policy to address in forthcoming years.

There are a number of acknowledgements which should be made. Many people have helped and offered encouragement. Colleagues have been supportive; the British Society of Gerontology Publications Committee has remained enthusiastic and steadfast. Our families have suffered an amount of preoccupation and unavailability; without their understanding the task would not have been possible. Finally, the support of our commissioning editor, Rosie Barker, has been invaluable. Our thanks to all for their assistance, in whatever form it was given.

Judith Phillips
Bridget Penhale

CHAPTER 1

Reviewing the Literature on Care Management

Judith Phillips

Introduction

Care management is a relatively recent concept in health and social care, yet since its introduction in the late 1970s it has received substantial attention from both academic and practice literature and has dominated social services agendas in the last decade as local authority social services departments struggle with its implementation in practice.

The literature on care management comes predominantly from three main sources. Much of the initial writing on the subject was introduced by the Personal Social Services Research Unit (PSSRU) at the University of Kent which transferred the idea from North America and refined it in its British context through a number of demonstration and pilot projects. This literature is optimistic and mainly academic. The Department of Health in the UK embraced many of the concepts developed by the PSSRU and since the early 1980s a plethora of literature has appeared from official sources in the form of both guidance documents and a series of evaluation reports. This literature has been predominantly prescriptive and provides advice on what care management is and how it can be implemented; consequently much of it is directed at senior managers. The third source of literature has been more critical of the concept and its application and is based on the difficulties in the translation of theory into practice and the success (or lack of it) of care management in different practice settings. This chapter gives a brief overview of the main issues addressed in the literature concerning care management. It is not intended to be exhaustive of the literature but aims to provide a framework for subsequent chapters.

The Introduction of Care Management

The concept of care management was developed in North America in the early 1970s primarily as a response to what was perceived as increasing fragmentation of services and the need for cost containment of service provision (Moxley 1989). Other significant influences leading to the perceived need for care management as a system included the process of deinstitutionalization and decentralization as people with multiple and complex needs required social support as they moved out into the community resulting principally from the closure of large scale institutions.

In American terms, care management could be defined as 'a client-level strategy for promoting the co-ordination of human services, opportunities or benefits' (Moxley 1989). The essential ingredients, therefore, were services tailor-made to the individual based on their own distinctive set of needs; the mobilizing of services and agencies to address similar packages of client goals to provide a consistent, integrated and co-ordinated response; and continuity of care both in relation to meeting the individual's needs at any one point and additionally over a period of time. As with the eventual adoption of the concept in the UK there was a strong focus on outcomes based on the above with many of the experiments and pilot projects focusing on long-term clients who were considered as otherwise vulnerable to entering residential care. This approach based on outcomes heavily concentrated on the financial and budgetary aspects as well as on the effectiveness of targeting.

Although a variety of other models exist, the 'social care entrepreneurship' model of care management with its concern for management of cost, which has been dominant in the United States was transferred to Britain (an alternative 'service brokerage model,' with a concentration on the task of advocacy, had been successfully used but primarily with physically disabled adults and people with a learning disability). The success of care management in the United States has not, however, been wholly proven; development of the practice of care management has been erratic and patchy. The concept still lacks clarity and the lack of adequate funding results in a questioning of its viability (Berkowitz 1992). Steinberg and Carter (1983) in their review of United States care management claim that it is effective as an intervention if aimed at longer term cases, although they admit that the circumstances of these people are not necessarily going to improve through intervention. In fact, to be successful in cost-effective terms, American experiments showed that two features were necessary: an extensive dependence on informal care and an integrated system of services. Care managers also needed to have control over the resources available to them. Callahan (1989) in reviewing a number of American projects found that costs were in fact increased through the introduction of care management.

Despite these difficulties the concept of care management was enthusiastically embraced by the Department of Health although clear differences existed in the application and operation of the American model in Britain. The United States has a wide diversity of population, disorganized and patchy social services provision and a vast number of private social care providers unlike Britain where state-run services still have an important presence in service provision. Transferring a concept which has little experience of operating within the public sector to Britain has led to difficulties in its application here as the American model seemed to relate more to a plurality of different providers. Huxley (1991) suggests that the government did not want to see any evaluative outcome of the American experiments indicating that a 'genuine improvement in the coordination of health and welfare services for the most vulnerable groups in society has not been the real objective' (p.366).

One of the main difficulties in transferring the concept has been the relegation of professional practice and values with project management being seen as the driving force behind its development in the United States (Orme and Glastonbury 1993).

Problems have also arisen in the definition and redefinition of care management since its transfer from the United States. Both here and in the United States early work referred to case-rather than care-management until the functions of care management were recognized as complex and wider than just a task of managing different cases or clients; it involved a range of activities, services and networks. The usage of the term case rather than care was also seen as demeaning to clients of the service, focusing on their weaknesses rather than their strengths (Onyett 1992). Some commentators (Payne 1995) would argue, however, that there is little distinction made in reality. A further distinction can be made between care management as a process and as a function. The process of care management has been emphasized in the Department of Health guidance and highlights both the planning and management elements of care management through assessment, care planning, reviewing and monitoring. The functions of the care manager go beyond this and can include social work, counselling and advocacy as well as care planning. The latter, however, have not been given as much weight as the former in the development of the concept in Britain.

Pilot Projects in the United Kingdom

A large body of research now exists on the time-limited demonstration and pilot projects set up in the early stages of care management in the UK, initially through the PSSRU. In 1970 the Kent (Thanet) Community Care Scheme was the showpiece for care management in this country and provided the model later adopted by the government. Other projects such as the Gloucester Care for the Elderly programme (Dant *et al*. 1989) where care managers were placed in primary health care settings without devolved budgets were not favoured as models to be replicated on a national basis. The essential features of the Kent (Thanet) project included experienced social workers with small caseloads and devolved budgets working with frail older people at risk of residential care. The budget, set at two-thirds the cost of a place in residential care, enabled social workers to access services in the independent and voluntary sectors as well as their own, and to cost each individual package of care. In comparison to a similar group of older people receiving traditional services, those in the experimental group fared better with the probability of admission to residential care halved and the probability of remaining at home doubled. The cost of care was also much lower than if residential care had been supplied as the alternate option (Challis and Davies 1986). As a preventative and cost saving approach it was impressive and similar schemes were extended into other urban areas of the country (Gateshead and Darlington).

The Darlington project included an evaluation of additional features of care management. Working in a multi-disciplinary team, clients' needs were assessed and packages of care from a variety of providers developed and reviewed. As well as the usual tasks of care management the care manager 'had to give considerable emotional support and advice to older people and their families as well as support home care assistants and resolve conflict in the care network' (Challis *et al.* 1995, p.10). The project was designed to provide home care to physically frail older people who would otherwise require long-stay hospital care. The outcomes were again reported as positive with, among others, an improvement in the overall morale and a reduction in apathy and depression among older people in the project compared to the control group, less distress among carers and a cost advantage in relation to long-stay hospital care (Challis *et al.* 1995).

Several critiques of these initial projects can be found in the literature. Means and Smith (1994) highlight three complications. In selecting the sample, problem clients (those with dementia or carers reluctant to share care) were filtered out; only frail older people were included leaving a question mark over the effectiveness of the approach for other groups of vulnerable elders. Lewis (1994) argues that if care managers in these experiments had been assigned to cases with lower levels of need, where the opportunity for substitution of residential care was less, then there would have been the possibility of rising costs. Payments to helpers were low and they were not considered as employees with entitlement to holidays and sick pay. The replication of the model was questionable because of the high profile and extra resources as well as the unusually lower caseloads held by the enthusiastic social workers engaged in the project which were unlikely to be adopted and experienced elsewhere. This has certainly been the case in other projects such as the Scarcroft project in York (Nocon 1994) where one of the main difficulties was the lack of time available to staff for care planning. Another was the difficulty in calculating costs as agencies used different costing methods. Fisher (1991) also argues that it is difficult to distinguish what was specifically beneficial about care management as the practice model is not defined by the researchers. 'The scheme does not provide an adequate basis for generalizing to a practice model of care management applicable to social services in general' (p.219).

Much of the research activity at PSSRU has been devoted to the resource implications of social care within what they term as the 'production of welfare' approach which links needs, resources and outcomes. 'Care management brings welfare objectives and resource constraints together and therefore has a pivotal role in the integration of social and economic criteria at the level of service provision where the balancing of needs and resources, scarcity and choice must take place' (Challis *et al*. 1995, p.20).

Their research was the first attempt to articulate the mixed economy on the ground. Cost has, therefore, been at the centre of this research (see Challis *et al*. 1989) which has tended to underrate other aspects of care management (Payne 1995). To some extent this reflects the background of those researchers as primarily economists. The publication of some of the research and the theoretical frameworks within which the production of welfare model is expressed take us into the world of micro-economics which can be inaccessible for many wishing to translate theory to practice.

Official Literature

Despite some of the criticisms of the early projects, the work of PSSRU on care management impressed Sir Roy Griffiths as a way of achieving his 'seamless service'. The approach suited the aims and philosophy of government policies regarding welfare and was subsequently introduced formally and on a national basis through the National Health Service and Community Care Act (1990).

Growing numbers of older people in the population with social care needs, escalating public sector expenditure following the growth in provision of private residential homes and the growing emphasis on home-based rather than institutional care provided the backdrop to the development of the community care changes and the introduction of care management. As in the United States, it was seen as a way to reduce costs, to provide a solution to bridge the gap between health and social care, to provide inter-agency collaboration and secure co-ordination between the burgeoning number of care agencies that the government expected would flourish under the new arrangements. It was perceived as essential to the effective handling of the mixed economy of welfare.

Care management was seen in the report produced by Sir Roy Griffiths for the government as forming part of the cornerstone of community care. It was to be targeted specifically at older people with complex and multiple needs. It was to be cost-effective and to promote the emphasis on living independently in the community. It was also seen to redress the critiques of the earlier decades of a lack of co-ordination in health and social care, fragmentation in services and the inflexibility of services which had been identified (Audit Commission 1986). Six objectives of care management and needs-led assessment were specified:

1. Ensuring that the resources available (including resources transferred from social security) are used in the most effective way to meet individual care needs.

2. Restoring and maintaining independence by enabling people to live in the community wherever possible.

3. Working to prevent or to minimize the effect of disability and illness in people of all ages.

4. Treating those who need services with respect and providing equal opportunities for all.

5. Promoting individual choice and self-determination, and building on existing strengths and care resources.

6. Promoting partnership between users, carers and service providers in all sectors, together with organizations of and for each group.

(Department of Health 1990, p.23)

Care management was seen as the principal means of putting policy into practice. The guidance that followed the White Paper and subsequent Act detailed the process through which this could be achieved (Care Management and Assessment: The Practitioners Guide/The Managers Guide, Department of Health 1991).

The functions of care management included providing information about available assistance, determining the level of assessment, the assessing of need, producing care plans, securing the necessary resources and services to implement the plans, monitoring the arrangements and reviewing the user's needs. The implementation of these eight core tasks was to be completed by April 1993. Of these, assessment was seen as the most vital; what came after was subsidiary to it. Although this was not a new function for social workers, the emphasis was placed more firmly on it being needs-led rather than service directed, and this was confirmed by placing it firmly within the purchasing function of social services. Knapp et al. (1992) argue that greater objectivity in decision-making and more accountability to clients would be achieved through this shift although others were more sceptical of the government's emphasis on assessment, seeing it as confirming the rationing function of care management (Westland 1991) and as a further attempt to redirect costs away from residential care (Payne 1995).

In carrying out the functions of care management and assessment, certain goals are to be achieved at both client and organizational level: choice, partnership, empowerment of users and carers, quality assurance and economy, effectiveness and efficiency. There remains an inherent contradiction and a tension, however, between these objectives. The translation of assessment into real tangible services can only take place within available resources and although partnership is encouraged, need still appears to be defined by service availability and the local authority rather than by individual clients. Empowerment remains, however, a strong feature in government rhetoric. This has been further emphasised in DOH sponsored reports (Smale et al. 1993) which emphasize the necessity to adopt the exchange model of assessment where users and carers are seen as experts in their own right about their own particular needs.

The translation of these ideals into practice has, however, been less than straightforward. Although one agency, local authorities were given the lead responsibility in implementing care management; its introduction is far from uniform and many different models exist. The wide variety of models in use, many introduced by the DHSS in 1983 as part of its 'Care in the Community' drive, have left many local authorities in uncertainty about which model to pursue. Huxley (1991) provides a comprehensive review of the theoretical (production of welfare), organisational (clinical, administrative and decentralised budgets) and content (casework, social skills and brokerage) models of care management. Similar categorization has been made in terms of the task by Biggs and Weinstein (1991) and Cambridge (1992) who have also identified at least seven different models ranging from a keyworker model akin to residential social work arrangements to a semi-independent care manager outside the public sector. In implementing these models, mainly from the top down, several authorities have been dominated by organizational restructuring rather than an explicit evaluation of models in practice.

Means and Smith (1994) argue that uncertainty remains within local authorities as to the place of care management within the new arrangements. Although on an individual basis care management is being realised, on a systems level there are dilemmas in relation to the identification of unmet need. Similarly, there are dilemmas as to who should be the care manager, at what level the budget should be held and at what level the purchaser/provider split should operate.

Further government-sponsored reports and publications relate to initial evaluations of care management. In January 1994 a study was carried out in seven local authorities on the way in which care management was being developed (Implementing Caring for People, DOH 1994). At this stage all authorities in the study were struggling to process the unexpected volume of work in relation to older people and particularly those with complex needs. In some cases this meant that providers were involved in assessments. Administrative workloads were also high and worry was expressed that care management resources were being spread too thinly. This was echoed again in a later study by the Social Services Inspectorate (Interim report, DOH and SSI 1993) which stressed that if the commitment was to involve users and carers then time was required for this along with acknowledgement from management in the allocation of cases. Both documents highlight the variability in practice not only between authorities but also within single authorities.

Social Work and Care Management: A Critique

The introduction of care management has been criticized by a number of commentators because it has led to an apparent devaluing of traditional social work skills and values. It is seen rather as a bureaucratic nightmare and is an impossible task given resource constraints. This third section turns its attention to some of these critical arguments put forward by both re-searchers and practitioners.

The actual nature of the relationship between social work and care management is less than clear. The Griffiths report (1988), subsequent legislation and the official guidance made very little mention of social work. Although it appears that social work is integral to care management, this was not explicitly stated and social work was denied any distinctive role. The role of the care manager was seen not as the exclusive domain of the social worker but allowed for a broadening of the role to include a variety of other professionals and disciplines. Some critics see this lack of clarity in the location of social work and the legislative bombardment that descended on social services departments as an attempt at the deconstruction of the social work profession (Payne 1995) and pauperization and marginalization of older people (Jack 1992). For some the very basis of social work was threatened and its value-base eroded.

In some respects the central tenets of care management are little different from what went before. Social work focus on advice and information giving, on practical help and on the role of the social worker as 'provider, locator, interpreter, mediator and aggressive intervener' suggested by Florence Hollis (1964, p.155) provide some continuity. More recently, Goldberg and Connelly's (1982) emphasis on the social worker as coordinator of services, resource person and community worker can all be translated into care management. Similarities can also be found in Reid and Shyne's (1969) development of task-centred social work and the concept of keyworking developed in the 1970s (Dant and Gearing 1990) which has parallels with the concept of partnership. Assessment processes too have traditionally been the 'bread and butter' of social work.

However, others would argue that 'any tendency to assert that the concept is merely old wine in new bottles must be firmly resisted' (Petch *et al.* 1994). There is a need to redefine roles, skills and tasks and to reassert social work's status within care management. Payne (1995) argues that social work is essential if care management is to succeed. Social work in the new system, however, differs from traditional social work. It is not intended to be used with all service users, but specifically with those people with the most complex needs; holistic needs-led assessment is stressed more than before with less emphasis on the medical model; one person co-ordinates the care package and there is a stronger emphasis on users and carers and their strengths. Finally, the delegation of budgets takes social workers into unfamiliar and rather uncomfortable territory as market mechanisms enter the professional–client relationship. Parton (1994) argues that it seems that social work no longer has the 'core underlying knowledge base and legitimacy' (p.101) to carry through the process of care management although he sees this more as a development illustrative of a post-modern society.

Several other tensions, ambiguities and dilemmas are highlighted in the literature. One of the initial concerns was that care management would be more about eligibility than need given the constraints within which services could be provided. Care management was more properly described as gatekeeping and rationing (Jack 1992) with need linked firmly to risk and dependency and hence resources (Lewis 1994). Yet again this is a traditional function of social work (Davies 1994); social workers are not new to these evident tensions within assessment, although the tendency to a service-led approach appears to have been unintentionally condoned by the development of lengthy check-list type assessment forms (Petch *et al.* 1994; Caldock and Nolan 1994).

Literature has also recently emerged critiquing the process of assessment and in particular the paperwork surrounding it, highlighting the length and inflexibility of the forms (Petch *et al.* 1994). A survey of 65 practitioners in Scotland found that forms seemed to become ends in themselves and also tended to disempower clients (MacDonald and Myers 1995). The fear expressed by social workers is that assessment will become a mechanical, bureaucratic process rather than serving client need.

Lying behind this is the concern that social work is being divided by one of the most radical changes in social work – the purchaser/provider split – with an erosion of traditional social work emphasis on counselling, establishing a relationship and providing ongoing support. Traditional counselling skills employed for purposes beyond assessment in a complex care package will, in all probability, now be contracted out. Social work practitioners feel uneasy and find it difficult to switch from a provider role to purely a purchasing position (MacDonald and Myers 1995). Continuity in their relationship with clients is eroded with uncertainty as to whether further reviews should be carried out by purchaser or provider. For many practitioners it seems as if social work has little role to play after the task of assessment is complete and assessment is viewed increasingly as a simple, 'one-off' event rather than a dynamic and on-going process.

The relationship between social workers, their clients and other professionals is also being challenged. Partnership with clients challenges professionalism and can lead to a conflict between worker and client in the definition of need (Petch *et al.* 1994). True partnership with the client might equally result in a conflict for the care manager with their employer. Smith *et al.* (1993) in a study of six community care projects found that issues of empowerment, quality and equal opportunities were not being addressed because of such difficulties. Social workers also appeared to be caught between client and manager with little freedom to shape their own practice (Howe 1991).

Biggs (1991) arguing from a psychodynamic perspective sees care management as ultimately unworkable as it views interpersonal relationships as unproblematic. An emphasis is placed on transactions at one point in time and these are seen as occurring in rational circumstances.

Multi-disciplinary assessment is also fraught with problems with evidence to suggest that the background of the assessor is influential in the definition of need. Petch *et al.* (1994), through the use of a videoed interview between a GP and an elderly person, found both similarities and differences between health and social work employees; needs relating to illness were discussed by medical staff but were not mentioned by the social worker or occupational therapist. Similar findings have been found in other studies (Caldock and Nolan 1994; Beardshaw and Towell 1990). Hoyes, Means and LeGrand (1992) found that responses depended on which agency received the initial request – if this came to the occupational therapy department it was defined as needing an occupational therapy response and probable service.

Inconsistency is also reported in terms of when care management is applied. Petch *et al.* (1994), in their review of Scottish arrangements, found that 'the basis for selection for care management was unclear, suggesting the absence of any shared concept' (p.3). There is a need, therefore, to clarify the concept and the definition of care management: who is it for; who does it benefit; in what circumstances is it most applicable.

In response to these criticisms and areas of uncertainty a growing body of training material on the skills required in care management has emerged. To carry out these new tasks social workers have to be skilled and trained in areas of unfamiliarity, namely budgetary skills and skills in working and negotiating with the independent sector (Phillips 1992). Greater skills are called for in working in partnership with clients (Stevenson and Parsloe 1993); interpersonal skills required for effective co-working and coordination (Hunter and Wistow 1991; Hughes 1993); creative problem-solving skills (Berkowitz 1992) along with computer skills. New attitudes to risk and accountability are also required. Developing such skills within an ethical and anti-discriminatory framework is also vital if social work is to have a basis in care management.

As the literature illustrates, care management in all its various forms is not a panacea for all but it does appear to have increased the status of older people on the welfare agenda, made social work accountable and provided opportunities for health and social care professionals to work together. Although the literature has been critical the advantages of care management are being highlighted and new agendas for its future development outlined. The following chapters of this book explore such agendas and draw on research findings to plug the gaps in our knowledge of care management, for example its success in meeting the needs of people from black and minority ethnic communities (Chapter 11).

References

Audit Commission (1986) *Making a Reality of Community Care*. London: HMSO.

Beardshaw, V. and Towell, D. (1990) *Assessment and Care Management: Implications for the Implementation of Caring for People*. London: Kings Fund Institute.

Berkowitz, N. (1992) 'Care management: an American perspective.' In S. Ramon (ed) *Care Management: Implications for Training*. Sheffield: Sheffield University/ATSWE.

Biggs, S. (1991) 'Community care, case management and the psychodynamic perspective.' *Journal of Social Work Practice 5*, 1, 71–81.

Biggs, S. and Wienstein, J. (1991) *Assessment, Case Management and Inspection in Community Care*. London: CCETSW.

Caldock, K. and Nolan, M. (1994) 'Assessment and community care: are the reforms working?' *Generations Review 4*, 4, 2–5.

Callahan, J. (1989) 'Case management for the elderly: a panacea?' *Journal of Ageing and Social Policy 1*, 1/2, 181–195.

Cambridge, P. (1992) 'Case management in community services: organisational responses.' *British Journal of Social Work 22*, 5, 495–517.

Challis, D. and Davies, B. (1986) *Case Management in Community Care*. Aldershot: Gower.

Challis, D., Darton, R., Johnson, L., Stone, M. and Traske, K. (1995) *Care Management and Health Care of Older People*. Aldershot, PSSRU: Arena.

Challis, D., Chesterman, J., Traske, K. and von Abendorff, R. (1989) 'Assessment and case management some cost implications.' *Social Work and Social Sciences Review 1*, 3, 147–163.

Dant, T., Carley, M., Gearing, B. and Johnson, M. (1989) *Co-ordinating Care: The Final Report of the Care of Elderly People at Home Project*. London: Policy Studies Institute and Open University Press.

Dant, T. and Gearing, B. (1990) 'Keyworkers for elderly people in the community: case managers and care co-ordinators.' *Journal of Social Policy 19*, 331–360.

Davies, M. (1994) *The Essential Social Worker* (3rd edition). Aldershot: Gower.

Department of Health (1990) *Community Care in the Next Decade and Beyond: Policy Guidance*. London: HMSO.

Department of Health (1991) *Care Management and Assessment: Practitioners' Guide*. London: HMSO.

Department of Health (1994) *Implementing Caring for People: Care Management*. Lancashire: Health Publications.

Department of Health/SSI (1993) *Inspection of Assessment and Care Management Arrangements in Social Services Departments*, Interim Overview Report. London: HMSO.

Fisher, M. (1991) 'Defining the practice content of care management.' *Social Work and Social Sciences Review 2*, 204–230.

Goldberg, T. and Connolly, N. (1982) *The Effectiveness of Social Care for the Elderly*. London, Policy Studies Institute: Heineman.

Griffiths Report (1988) *Community Care: An Agenda for Action*. London: HMSO

Hollis, F. (1964) *Casework: A Psychosocial Therapy*. New York: Random House Press.

Howe, D. (1991) 'The family and the therapist: towards a sociology of social work method.' In M. Davies (ed) *The Sociology of Social Work*. London: Routledge.

Hoyes, L., Means. R. and LeGrand, J. (1992) *Made to Measure? Performance Measurement and Community Care*. Bristol: Bristol School of Advanced Urban Studies, Occasional Paper 39.

Hughes, B. (1993) 'Assessment of older people and their carers.' *British Journal of Social Work 23*, 4, 345–365.

Hunter, D. and Wistow, G. (1991) *Elderly People's Integrated Care System (EPICS): An Organisational, Policy and Practice Review*. Leeds: Nuffield Institute for Health, Report no.3.

Huxley, P. (1991) 'Effective case management for mentally ill people: the relevance of recent evidence from the USA for case management services in the United Kingdom.' *Social Work and Social Sciences Review 2*, 3, 192–204.

Jack, R. (1992) 'Case management and social services: welfare or trade fare?' *Generations Review 2*, 1, 4–7.

Knapp, M., Cambridge, P., Thomason, C., Beecham, J., Allen, C. and Darton, R. (1992) *Care in the Community: Challenge and demonstration*. Canterbury: PSSRU.

Lewis, J. (1994) 'Care management and the social services: reconciling the irreconcilable.' *Generations Review 4*, 1, 2–4.

MacDonald, C. and Myers, F. (1995) *Assessment and Care Management: The Practitioner Speaks*. Community Care in Scotland discussion Paper No.5: University of Stirling.

Means, R. and Smith, R. (1994) *Community Care. Policy and Practice*. London: Macmillan.

Moxley, D. (1989) *The Practice of Case Management*. New York: Sage.

Nocon, A. (1994) *Collaboration in Community care in the 1990s*. Newcastle: Business Education Publishers.

Onyett, S. (1992) *Case Management in Mental Health*. London: Chapman and Hall.

Orme, J. and Glastonbury, B. (1993) *Care Management*. London: Macmillan.

Parton, N. (1994) 'The nature of social work under conditions of (post) modernity.' *Social Work and Social Sciences Review 5*, 2, 93–113.

Payne, M. (1995) *Social Work and Community Care*. London: Macmillan.

Petch, A., Stalker, K., Taylor, C. and Taylor, J. (1994) *Assessment and Care Management Pilot Projects in Scotland: An Overview*. Stirling: Community care in Scotland Discussion Papers, University of Stirling.

Phillips, J. (1992) 'The future of social work with older people.' *Generations Review 2*, 4, 12–15.

Reid, W. and Shyne, A. (1969) *Brief and Extended Casework*. New York: Columbia University Press.

Smale, G., Tuson, G., with Biehal, N. and Marsh, P. (1993) *Empowerment, Assessment, Care Management and the Skilled Worker*. London. National Institute for Social Work: HMSO.

Smith, R., Gaster, L., Harrison, L., Martin, L., Means, R. and Thistlethwaite, P. (1993) *Working Together for Better Community Care*. Bristol: SAUS.

Steinberg, R. and Carter, G. (1983) *Case Management and the Elderly*. New York: Lexington Books.

Stevenson, O. and Parsloe, P. (1993) *Community Care and Empowerment*. York: Joseph Rowntree Foundation.

Westland, P. (1991) 'The community health services: a new relationship.' In I. Allen (ed) *Health and Social Services: The New Relationship*. London: Policy Studies Institute.

CHAPTER 2

New Concepts, Old Responses
Assessment and Care Management
Pilot Projects in Scotland

Alison Petch[1]

Introduction

In the twelve months prior to April 1993 a number of evaluations were conducted on pilot projects established to explore various aspects of the community care reforms. This comprises the first phase of a continuing programme of evaluation of the implementation of the new community care arrangements in Scotland. Four pilot areas were involved (Table 2.1), ranging from a multi-disciplinary assessment group centred on a health centre in the Borders to an elderly team in Fife which represented the intended pattern of reorganization across the region. It should be noted that in Tayside there were in fact four individual pilots within the study, varying by care group and in detailed arrangements.

The focus of the evaluation differed in each of the four regions but included aspects of the assessment process, the primary concern at that stage, in all areas. In Tayside, where there was a substantial in-house evaluation, it was the views of the assessors, in particular on the proforma, that were sought. In Fife (Cupar) the detail of screening was highlighted, and in Central (Alva) the selection of cases for care management. Multi-disciplinary assessment provided the impetus in Borders (Duns), with a pilot assessment group established in a primary health care setting. This chapter will select across these projects to comment on three key concepts: screening, needs-based assessment and care management. It should be stressed that in all areas the analysis and commentary refers only to the period during which the pilot projects were being evaluated. In several cases practice has been refined or indeed more radically altered at a subsequent date. The commentary should not, therefore, be taken as indicative of current practice in these areas. The focus is on principles rather than the detail of local practice as it

1   This paper draws upon work completed by colleagues at the Social Work Research Centre – Kirsten Stalker, Cathy Taylor and Julie Taylor. Their invaluable contribution is gratefully acknowledged.

Table 2.1 Pilot Projects

Tayside		
4 pilots of different models of care management	views of assessor	semi-structured interviews with assessors
		video exercise
Fife		
elderly specialist team	screening and assessment processes	observation
		case monitoring forms
		semi-structured interviews with staff
Central		
specialist community careteam operating alongsidea children and families team	selection for care management	observation
	experience of users	case monitoring form
		semi-structured interviews with care managers and users
Borders		
multidisciplinary healthcentre based pilot for assessment of elderly people	multidisciplinary assessment group	observation
		case monitoring form
		questionnaires and interview schedule
		video exercise

occurred either during the pilot project or, indeed, has subsequently developed.

Screening

Screening mechanisms have an important function in the delivery of social care. There are significant variations in need between different individuals, ranging from those that require relatively straightforward help in the form of advice and information to those with complex needs requiring a detailed and complex assessment. The process of screening seeks to identify the level of help appropriate to individual needs. Despite, however, positing six potential levels of assessment, the official guidance (Social Services Inspectorate/Social Work Services Group 1991a; 1991b) says little about the bridging process between the initial referral and entry to assessment. How that response is organized is left for individual authorities to decide. The earlier White Paper 'Caring for People' comments that '…local authorities will need to form their own views about when a formalized assessment process becomes necessary…' (p.18). The Scottish Office Guidance (1991) is no more prescriptive on the matter; in regard to screening they urge authorities that '…procedures should be sufficiently comprehensive and flexible to cope with a wide variety of need presented in many different ways…' (s5.2).

The screening process was a particular feature of the Cupar evaluation in Fife. In an attempt to meet their aim of developing more accessible services, Fife sought to establish a network of Community Access Points (CAPs). In the first instance these have been located at the major social work offices ('hub' offices) but the intention was that 'satellite' sites should operate on a sessional basis throughout the communities. The purpose of CAPs is two-fold: to provide a first point of contact for anyone requiring information, support or guidance about any social work, council or voluntary sector service and to adopt a community development role.

Figure 2.1 details the referral route for all initial enquiries to the Elderly Specialist Team (EST) in Cupar. It should be noted that the route is unidirectional: enquiries processed by the EST cannot be redirected to the CAP, while referrals passed from the CAP to the EST cannot be referred back. The routes travelled by the 112 initial enquiries monitored over a two-month period can be traced. The bulk of enquiries (85%) were dealt with by either the CAP (40) or direct through the duty system to the EST (55); home care managers recorded over half of the remaining enquiries (a total of 17 to 'other').

The significant differences are in the referrers who use the two main routes. Health professionals account for one-third of initial enquiries, while self or a friend or relative acting on behalf of the individual constitute a further 28 per cent of enquiries. Whereas almost 60 per cent of the former enquiries were directed to the EST, only 31 per cent of those from self or family took this route. Conversely, two-thirds of the later group went to the CAP compared to only 27 per cent of the health professionals' referrals. Individuals referred by health professionals, regardless of who recorded the enquiry, were highly likely to be allocated for assessment. Thus 51 of the 55 enquiries going direct moved forward for assessment compared to only 19 of the 40 to the CAP.

The pattern of enquiries that emerged in practice suggested that the screening role envisaged for the CAP has been only partially successful. Many professionals are approaching the EST directly and team members are therefore having to deal from the beginning with cases where they would have expected some initial investigation to have been done by the CAP. Rather than social work time being freed up by a screening mechanism, the amount of duty time had increased dramatically. There were 'phone calls all

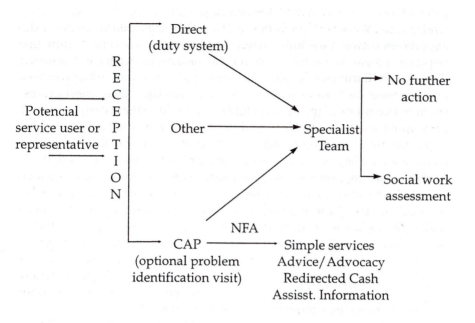

Figure 2.1 Cupar – Referral Pathway

day', 'referrals came direct without any filtering', there 'shouldn't be any need to pass on basic enquiries'. A particular problem with direct referrals to the EST at this stage was the inability, as computer terminals were not yet available, to perform an initial record check to determine whether the referral was a known case, actively being worked with or not.

Expectations on the part of the EST that the CAP would function as a total intake system, thereby screening all enquiries, have not been met in practice. As the system has evolved health professionals in particular have bypassed the CAP point of entry. For the CAP team, moreover, there are tensions in the balance of their role between handling initial enquiries and promoting community development. Such factors have important implications in terms of equality of access and of equity of treatment. CAP enquiries, for example, had far less detail recorded, perhaps partly because of an ideology of declientization. Incomplete referral forms generated critical comment when passed to the EST – 'so much time is tied up finding out details that should have been on the referral form'. More critically, those enquiries directed to the EST enter only one filter, the team manager, who then decides whether the case should be allocated, whereas those to the CAP face two filtering mechanisms. On the other hand, referrals direct to the EST have bypassed, irrevocably, the range of possible options offered, at least in theory, by community access.

A not dissimilar feature was evident in the Alva pilot project in Central region. Here an innovative dual duty system was established which took referrals for both the Adult Services Team (AST) and the Children and Families Team (CFT). A duty worker from one of the teams was available each day, but with appointments available only on three days of the week, telephone cover being provided on the intervening days. All referrals, regardless of the worker's recommendation, were passed to the appropriate team manager for closure or allocation. Team managers were also, however, the first point of contact for almost half the referrals in their respective teams (49% in CFT, 45% in AST). Just under 40 per cent of all enquiries were generated by other professionals – GPs, health professionals, hospital or social work department – who, it appeared, either bypassed the duty system direct to the team manager or knew when a worker from the relevant team was on duty. This practice of bypassing the screening mechanism has gradually been discouraged both by 'educating' other professionals as to the operation of the new system and re-routing the referral back through the duty worker.

Needs-Based Assessment

The driving and fundamental parameter of needs-based assessment has been comprehensively promoted: '…care management and assessment emphasize adapting services to needs rather than fitting people into existing services, and dealing with the needs of individuals as a whole rather than assessing needs separately for different services…' (SSI/SWSG 1991a, 11). There has, however, perhaps been less consideration of the process necessary for individual workers to transform their practice. Evidence was available from a number of the pilots on the extent to which needs-led assessment was evident in routine work.

In Fife, for example, case recording forms were completed for 53 cases allocated for assessment, with workers asked to state the user's main needs (up to three, although some reported more). Table 2.2 summarises the responses; a separation into needs-led and service-led has been imposed by the researcher. The division is somewhat arbitrary as it was not possible to impose a straightforward dichotomy due to the subjective nature of some of the 'needs', witness 'prompting', 'guidance' and 'control'. Such examples would appear to reflect the opinion of the worker rather than a user perspective; they have been included under 'needs-led' as they represent some shift from needs expressed as services. Nonetheless it can be seen that over half of the main needs remain expressed in service terms.

Table 2.2 Cupar – Main Needs

Service-Led		Needs-Led	
Respite	17	Social Contact	14
Assessment (psychiatric)	5	Personal Care	4
Day Care	4	24hr Care	4
Support/residential		Carers a break/support	2
Accommodation	3	Daily Support	2
Volunteer Help	3	Care of Pets	1
Counselling	2	Assistance in Home	1
Home Help	1	Support financially	1
Advice/benefits	1		
Alzheimers Support	1	?	
Advice on Services	1	Reassurance	3
Assessment (physical)	1	Prompting	2
		Guidance	1
?		Control	1
Medical Care/Support	3	Motivation	1
		Rehabilitation	1
Total	**42**	**Total**	**42**
(? = unclear/uncertain)			

A particular concern in this region was the extent to which the structure of the assessment form condoned a traditional service-led response. Thus, the assessment form was eighteen pages in length and comprised fourteen sections. Instructions specifically indicated which sections were to be completed according to the service to be provided:

- Day care Initial three pages + B,C,D,E,F.
- Respite Initial three pages + B,C,D,E,F,H,J.
- Part IV Initial three pages of RDL2 + all of assessment form.

Such directives would appear to conflict fundamentally with a needs-led approach.

Further empirical evidence on this central issue is available from the evaluation of the Duns pilot project in Borders. Full social care assessments were completed on 33 individuals. For the 29 cases where needs were identified, Table 2.3 separates out those needs which were expressed in terms of a service and those which were not. From a total of 61 needs, a large majority (72%) were expressed in terms of a service. The largest single group was for aids and adaptations (n=22), with the next largest, four for home care, well below. A range of other services, from day hospital to Border alarm, were recorded either once or twice.

Table 2.3 Duns – Recording of Needs

How needs were expressed	No. of needs	% of needs
Needs expressed in terms of a service	44	72%
Needs not expressed in terms of a service	17	28%
Total needs recorded	61	100%
(n = 29)		

A particular interest must be whether the assessment of need is influenced by the background of the assessor. The multi-disciplinary nature of the Duns pilot allowed comparison of the first need prioritized by four different professional groups across 32 cases. Table 2.4 demonstrates that across the 12 different needs recorded, the pattern of identification by different disciplines varied. Most notably, of the 12 occupational therapists, 11 formulated the elderly person's needs in terms of aids and adaptations. The other professionals recorded less uniform needs and there was far less emphasis on aids and adaptations. An analysis of the second to fourth prioritized needs of the elderly person revealed a similar pattern. The only other needs identified by three occupational therapists were help with the garden, a letter to housing and improved mobility. In the identification of care plans, likewise, there was variation between the groups. Twenty-two different care

**Table 2.4 Duns – First Prioritized Needs
Identified According to Discipline**

8 Social Workers		12 Occupational Therapists	
Aids/adaptations	= 2	Aids/adaptations	= 11
O.T. assessment	= 1	To call someone	
Home care	= 1	in an emergency	= 1
Day hospital for physiotherapist	= 1		
Border alarm	= 1		
Financial assistance	= 1		
No information	= 1		

6 Nurses		6 Home Care Organisers	
Border alarm	= 2	No information	= 2
Support/counselling	= 1	Day centre	= 1
Aids/adaptations	= 1	Relief for housekeeper	= 1
Help with hygiene	= 1	Help with housework	= 1
No information	= 1	Aids/adaptations	= 1

Table 2.5 Duns Needs and Care Plans

O.T.	S.W.	C.P.N.	C.N.S.	D.H.N
Needs				
aids/adaptations	alarm	health review	help shopping	domestic support
C.P.N.	family relatives	emotional support	company	social support
company	support/counselling	company	check hearing	Macmillan nurse
home care	home care	check hearing	family relatives	District nurse
Care Plans				
aids/adaptations	alarm	none recorded	home care	home care
C.P.N.	counselling	none recorded	health team	day hospital
company	home care	none recorded	Macmillan nurse	Macmillan nurse
home care	—	none recorded	SW for counselling	District nurse

plans were identified by the four disciplines on the assessment form. Of these, occupational therapists identified only aids/adaptations for seven and aids and a Border alarm for another. The other three disciplines identified a greater number and a larger variety of plans. Nursing staff identified 17 care plans (14 different ones) for six elderly people, social workers 12 care plans (10 different) for eight individuals, and home care organisers seven plans (five different) for six individuals.

Such differences in needs and care plans may, however, have reflected variations in the cases being assessed. In both Borders and Tayside, therefore, a video exercise was undertaken to explore to what extent differences would emerge amongst assessors in relation to the same case. Assessors from different disciplines were asked to watch a 25 minute video of an interview between an elderly lady and her GP and then to complete the assessment form used in their region, together with a questionnaire. A discussion was also held, which in Borders took the form of a case conference.

In Borders five assessors were involved – occupational therapist, social worker, community psychiatric nurse, community nursing sister and day hospital nurse – and Table 2.5 identifies the needs and care plans which were identified by these individuals. Fifteen different needs were identified, with the first priority need of each of the assessors being different. There was considerable difference between care plans, with, as for the live assessments above, a close correspondence between care plans and needs.

Table 2.6 Duns – Identification of Needs by Assessors

Day hospital nurse	A	B	C	D				
Community psychiatric nurse		B	C					H
Community nursing sister		B	C		E	F		
Occupational therapist					E		G	H
Social worker	A						G	H

Key
A = Domestic help   E = Company and stimulation
B = Family relationships   F = Counselling and support from social work
C = Nursing   G = Washing/dressing
D = Day Care   H = Mental health problems

In the subsequent group discussion the needs outlined in Table 2.6 were highlighted. There are both differences and similarities between health and social work employees in the perception of the client's needs. Amongst the differences were:

- Needs relating to illness were discussed by medical staff; they were not mentioned by social worker and occupational therapist.
- Likewise, although not anticipated, only medical staff mentioned family relationships.
- Only the occupational therapist and social worker focused on washing and dressing; no medical staff regarded this as a problem.

On other issues there was overlap:

- The community psychiatric nurse, occupational therapist and social worker expressed concern about the client's mental health problems. They discussed her depression and the risk of suicide. One said she was a 'very risky person'. The social worker noted that the client had tried to kill herself.
- The day hospital nurse and the social worker were the only two who indicated the need for domestic help.
- The community nurse and occupational therapist noted the need for company and stimulation. In one worker's view the client was 'screaming out for mental stimulation and company', yet this was not mentioned by the other three workers.

Taken in conjunction with the evidence across the assessments outlined above it would appear that elderly people were having different needs identified by different assessors. Moreover, the video exercise demonstrated that such differences were located both within and between health and social work. This is not to deny the opportunity for very different responses to the same set of needs but there must be a comprehensive, holistic recognition of these needs at an initial stage.

In the similar video exercise in Tayside, care managers in two of the pilot projects completed the assessment proformas following a viewing of the video. Of the ten care managers, seven had a social work background while the others had previously held posts as a district nurse, occupational therapist or senior home help organiser. In terms of the needs that were identified, eight of the ten spoke of the need for help with heavy housework, and five of the need for company and social contact. A range of other needs, however, were mentioned by only one or two individuals, ranging from mental stimulation and resolution of family problems to medical care and support and possible help with self-care and cooking. There was, therefore, little consensus. Although it can be argued that in a live situation further detail would be sought, nonetheless questions must again be raised about the variability apparent between assessors, be they from the same or different professions. Interviews with a small number of users in Central allowed an additional perspective to be brought into play, namely the extent to which the needs identified by care managers corresponded to those perceived by service users. Sixty-two per cent of respondents' perceived needs were also identified by care managers, and, conversely, 66 per cent of those identified by the latter were expressed by respondents. The areas of need identified by users but not echoed by care managers were health related, a finding in accord with that from Borders above.

Care Management

Much guidance has been devoted to the different models of care management and to the nature of cases appropriate for care management. To date, however, we know comparatively little of care management in routine operation. In the Central pilot, however, it was possible to scrutinize those cases defined as in receipt of care management and to compare their characteristics with cases where care management was not deemed to be necessary. Information was drawn in the main from case recording forms completed at the initial assessment (n=123) and six weeks later or on case closure (n=119). The initial forms identify 20 of the cases as potential candidates for care management. The second form shows that in the event 14 of the 20, plus one not originally identified, did go on to receive care management; six did not.

Three indicators **for** care management were selected and charted across the cases: the number of assessed problems, the degree of estimated risk and the identified needs. As with the indicators of care management outlined below, selection of specific items was made in line with criteria specified in the official guidance. The number of problems isolated ranged from none (12%) to fifteen, with just over a third having between one and three, a further 40 per cent between four and six, and the remainder (15%) over six. The seriousness of risk was classified as immediate, intervention needed, or at no risk. Identified needs ranged between none and three (75% with only one recorded) and were classified into categories of physical, emotional, social, practical, housing and other. Moreover an attempt was made to distinguish simple needs (69%) from those that were likely to be more complex (31%). On the basis of these three indicators four sub-groups were identified:

1. **negative:** those cases that show all three negative indicators for care management, i.e. few problems (less than three), no estimated risk, with simple needs (n=34; CM=1)

2. **borderline negative:** where two negative indicators are present, e.g. few problems, simple needs, but estimated to require intervention (n=53; CM=2)

3. **borderline positive:** those cases which are recorded as having only one negative indicator and two positive for care management (n=25; CM=8)

4. **positive:** cases which demonstrate all three positive indicators for care management, i.e. multiple problems (over three), estimated to be at immediate risk, with (possibly) complex needs (n=11; CM=4).

On this basis it appeared that 24 additional cases could potentially have been considered candidates for care management.

A similar exercise was then undertaken identifying from the six-week forms indicators **of** care management. These included the number and type of professional activities, the number of support services in place, support for users and carers, liaison with other agencies and care planning. Criteria for identification as negative or positive were then set, three being the cut-off for all indicators save contact with users where the negative criterion was less than once a fortnight. A maximum of five possible indicators of care management were therefore located, with over half of all the care managed cases (8) having three or four positive indicators. This compared with only two of the 104 non-care managed cases.

Tables 2.7 and 2.8 attempt to marry the two sets of indicators (**for** and **of**) for both care managed and non care managed cases. Table 2.7 demonstrates that just under half (seven) of the care managed cases show positive indicators both for and of care management. A further five cases, whilst appearing suitable for selection, show few key features (two or less) of the care management process.

Table 2.7 Alva – Indicators of and for Care Management – Care Managed Cases

Indicators for Care Management	Indicators of Care Management				
	4	3	2	1	Total
0 Negative	–	1	–	–	1
+1 Borderline negative	–	–	2	–	2
+2 Borderline positive	3	2	2	1	8
+3 Positive	1	1	2	–	4
Total	**4**	**4**	**6**	**1**	**15**

(max=5)

Two of the remaining three cases show few indicators either for or of care management, whilst the final case, although demonstrating no indicators in favour, appears to be receiving care management. From Table 2.8 it can be seen that of the 24 cases which were identified as potential candidates for care management, only two now show three or more positive indicators of care management. A further 14 show some positive indicators (up to two), whilst seven have none.

Table 2.8 Alva – Indicators of and for Care Management –
Non Care Managed Cases

Indicators for Care Management	Indicators of Care Management					
	4	3	2	1	0	Total
0 Negative	–	–	1	5	24	30
+1 Borderline negative	–	–	11	18	22	51
+2 Borderline positive	1	1	2	7	5	16
+3 Positive	–	–	2	3	2	7
Total	1	1	16	33	53	104

(max=5)

It has to be concluded from the above that in this particular pilot area the basis on which care managed cases was selected was unclear. Thus, for example, on the basis of the three indicators for care management, eleven cases were identified, only four of which were actually selected for care management. On the other hand two cases selected for care management demonstrated neither indicators for nor evidence of its occurrence in practice. A further case did not evidence any need for care management but appeared to be receiving it. Whilst acknowledging potential limitations in the case recording form as a data collection form, nonetheless the lack of a shared concept of care management within this team cannot be avoided. Such a conclusion was confirmed by further analysis of the eleven care managed cases where additional user interview material was available. Five rather than three indicators for care management were selected, together with eight indicators denoting care management in practice. Analysis suggested that whilst the majority of the eleven cases were appropriate for care management, one was not and three were doubtful. Likewise, in terms of care management actually being pursued, seven were good examples with many of the expected features in place, two displayed few features of care management and two, with only one or two features, could not in fact be said to be care managed.

The team which forms the subject of this analysis acknowledged difficulty in reaching common criteria for care management; they preferred rather to talk of care management as a process, with individual cases tapping in to the process at appropriate points. Moreover, there may not be a specific decision concerning which case gains entry to care management; rather, a worker may find herself carrying out certain activities which correspond to the care management process. When such a process, however, leads to the lack of clarity revealed above, it is difficult to support on grounds of equity or logic. Moreover, it flies in the face of the SSI/SWSG guidance which suggests: '...whatever groups are targeted [for care management] the criteria for selecting them should be understood by all staff, the other care agencies and by the public at large...' (1991a, 3.9).

The difficulties of implementing care management, particularly in the multi- disciplinary team, have been highlighted by Beardshaw and Towell (1990). Drawing upon earlier pilots they found that in the multi-disciplinary setting interpretations of the care manager role were influenced by the professional background of individuals. The broad definition of the role creates a climate where individual interpretation and emphasis may flourish, even, by default, be necessary. The implementation outlined above suggests that, as with the processes of screening and assessment, the transition to new modes of working requires much more than legislative intent and the repetition of a new vocabulary. Further research at the Social Work Research Centre will explore to what extent new responses emerge as the routine phase of implementation proceeds.

References

Beardshaw, V. and Towell, D. (1990) *Assessment and Care Management: Implications for the Implementation of Caring for People.* London: King's Fund Institute.

Department of Health (1989) *Caring for People: community care in the Next Decade and Beyond.* London: HMSO.

Scottish Office (1991) *Assessment and Care Management.* Circular SW11/1991.

SSI/SWSG (1991a) *Care Management and Assessment: Managers' Guide.* London: HMSO.

SSI/SWSG (1991b) *Care Management and Assessment: Practitioners' Guide.* HMSO.

CHAPTER 3

Multi-Disciplinary Assessment and Care Management

Kerry Caldock

Introduction

Government policy on community care as reflected in the 1989 White Paper and subsequent guidance documents emphasizes the pivotal role of multi-disciplinary assessment/working and care management. The success of the reforms will be largely contingent upon the working feasibility and efficacy of these processes. However, government exhortations to agencies and professions to work together have a long and undistinguished history. Hunter and Wistow (1991) sum up the literature on collaborative working thus:

> One reading of the recent history of most, if not all categories of joint activity would suggest it to be a chimera: a self-defeating illusion. In practice, it might be argued, inter-agency and inter-professional relationships have been more generally marked by conflict or stand-off rather than productive co-operation. (p.2)

In viewing the new assessment and subsequent care management arrangements – seen as being: a timely multi-agency, multi-disciplinary process (Department of Health 1989) – as the cornerstones of the community care reforms, it can be argued that assumptions have been made about multi-disciplinary functioning between and within agencies for which little precedent exists. Indeed, Hudson (1992) suggests that the government have been breezily optimistic in their references to working together in this way.

Whilst multi-agency/disciplinary functioning presents one set of problems for the community care reforms, a second set of factors vital to their success concerns the ways in which assessment is conceptualized within and between disciplines, with particular regard to the long-standing differences in perspective between social and medical models of care. Since it is generally accepted that effective care management can only be achieved following an appropriate and sufficiently broad assessment, the main focus of this chapter will be upon multi-disciplinary assessment. However, it should be borne in mind that the factors described as impacting upon joint working in assessment will, by virtue of the centrality of assessment to the whole process of community care, similarly affect care management.

The chapter will thus examine some of the differences in the ways assessment is conceptualized and practised and the possible impact of these factors on the progress of the reforms for which multi-disciplinary assessment and care management are pivotal.

Assessment: Background

The White Paper reforms tacitly acknowledged and attempted to address some of the difficulties with assessment which had been identified over the years. These included: uncertainty about the nature and purpose of assessment; assessments determined by the professional interest of the assessor (Allen, Hogg and Peace 1992; Ellis 1993); that assessment is not a precise or definitive process (DHSS 1985); that assessment led to a tendency to offer what was available rather than what was needed (Allen et al. 1992; Ellis 1993).

Compounding these difficulties with assessment is a lack of consensus on the meaning of need and how this relates to needs assessment (Baldwin 1986); and the likelihood that separate professional cultures and perspectives may prevent the objective assessment of client needs (Ellis 1993). The process of needs assessment has thus remained largely undefined and idiosyncratic. Fundamentally, the central problem appears to be a lack of agreed definitions, parameters and objectives for assessment within and between agencies. Confusion among health and social services staff about who would be doing assessment, what it would entail, and a lack of clarity or agreement about its objectives has been identified by a number of authors (Beardshaw and Towell 1990; Rowbottom 1992; Ellis 1993).

Whilst the White Paper and subsequent guidance documents, in taking up the theme of care management, have gone a long way to addressing long-standing problems of service fragmentation and lack of single accountable individuals whom users may contact, other more fundamental and explicit definitions and guidance about assessment *per se* were lacking. Following the White Paper, separate professional groupings, agencies and authorities have each developed their own documentation and criteria. Whilst some of this development has been of a collaborative and multi-disciplinary nature, much has not. Ellis (1993) had cautionary words to say about the dangers of focusing on the instruments of assessment rather than the process itself:

'In implementing the NHS and Community Care Act, the danger is that social services departments will concentrate their efforts on service criteria and pro-formas. Developing the tools of assessment will doubtless be perceived as a less difficult task than challenging the values and attitudes deeply embedded in assessment practice' (p.39).

There is evidence, Ellis contends, to indicate that practitioners readily incorporate into their formal practice assessment guidelines, pro-formas and prioritization criteria in a way which is designed to protect professional interests as much as promote those of users and carers. It may be that this issue will prove to be a major focus of research interest as the reforms continue, as it is likely to be 'where the action is at' in attempts to successfully implement multi-disciplinary assessment and care management practices.

Social and Medical Models of Care

It has been argued (Caldock 1992), that social workers and community care practitioners feel that medical opinions about care needs have prevailed even when social care was the priority. They expressed anxieties about 'sticking their necks out' to support the wishes of clients lest an unfavourable outcome such as a fall or injury (from rejecting residential care) lead to recrimination and a weakening of their position in future cases. Caldock and Nolan (1994) found that social services staff felt strongly that health services staff had a poor understanding of the principles of multi-disciplinary assessment and showed little commitment to it. Such criticisms were most often directed towards medical staff in both hospitals and general practice. As GPs are seen as having a 'pivotal' role in the reforms, this is clearly cause for concern. Medical staff were often cited as being least likely to fill out multi-disciplinary assessment documentation.

After the Seebohm report (1968) it was clearly established that the diagnosis of 'social problems' was the province of social workers and not doctors. Stacey (1988) moves on from this point to note that historically there has been a great deal of antagonism between doctors and social workers. Taking the case of child abuse (Dingwall, Eekelaar and Murray 1983) as an example, Stacey (1988) concludes that the different concepts of health and welfare and the different organisational structure of the health and social services may conspire to fail to protect children. It could be argued that the same dynamics working through assessments may affect the protection of elderly peoples' civil liberties and right to decide upon what risk they see as acceptable rather than what professionals are prepared to risk. This argument has been addressed by others (Norman 1980; Poyner and Hughes 1978) who have shown that moving people out of their homes and into residential care for their own safety (often for medical reasons) may have the opposite effect and increase the likelihood of death, especially in the first three months after the move. Indeed, Lieberman (1974) has suggested that the more a person appears to be at risk where they are, the worse will be their prognosis if moved.

Allen, Hogg and Peace (1992) found that pressure from relatives upon elderly people to enter residential care occurred frequently. They noted that in about 20 per cent of the cases they examined, there was clear pressure on elderly people to enter care without a crisis or a deterioration. They also point out that it often appeared that the pressure had been sanctioned or 'legitimised' by professionals who had intervened to support the choice of carers.

At a more fundamental level, there may also be a need to question whether the primacy of a medicalized view of elderly peoples' life situations in some assessment situations (e.g. hospital settings) is appropriate. Many elderly people suffer from multiple pathologies which, in conjunction with advanced age, would lead to a poor prognosis in the longer term. In assessment, other aspects of the lifestyles and wishes of older people should perhaps be accorded precedence over, and seen as more important than, a specific set of, 'disease labels' despite what may be perceived as health risks.

Nolan and Grant (1992) point out the tension between the implicitly curative orientation of acute geriatric care and the more holistic needs of an increasingly large section of the user population. They note that in the medical model there can be little doubt that clinical and rehabilitative functions are seen as more prestigious than the social and preventive (Wilkin and Hughes 1986).

There are, of course, a great many situations where the primacy of health problems and the importance of proper medical assessment and treatment are clear. This has become particularly important as it has been realised that many of the 'diseases of old age' do not lead to inevitable decline but are treatable and worthy of full medical attention.

The legitimacy of a medical model is not, as such, challenged. What is challenged is the often automatic and inappropriate application of the model. The primacy of the medical model over social care models may lead to an unbalanced focus upon illness, dependency and risk, rather than permitting the proper assessment of an individual's determination to adapt, cope, take risks and make choices – and accept the consequences of those choices. Indeed, much of the new assessment documentation following the reforms appears to continue to place a heavy emphasis on functional capabilities, ADL (Activities of Daily Living), problems and dependencies.

Medicalized views of care needs could act as a factor undermining the new primacy of community care and could also result in the persistence of inter-professional conflict, especially at the boundaries and interface of health and social care. It is apparent that if practitioners, from whatever agency or profession, lack clear frameworks or agreed understandings about what assessment comprises, the opportunities for misunderstanding and service fragmentation are greatly magnified and may serve to undermine co-operative and multi-disciplinary working.

Assessment: Professional and User Perspectives

There is a long history of research pointing out the divergence of perceptions of need held by users and professional providers in social services (Mayer and Timms 1970; Sainsbury 1980; Fisher 1989; Sinclair and Williams 1990).

However, despite the rhetoric that places emphasis on user choice, participation and needs-led approaches, Lloyd (1991) argues:

> A bottom-up approach which stresses the right of elderly individuals
> or consumers to services, to express their needs and have a say in the
> selection of services offered, to control their delivery and to protest
> when things go wrong is incompatible with the top-down approach
> with management assessing needs and deciding who is most needy,
> allocating scarce resources, rationed by a limitation on funding and
> adopting a professional stance before the dependent recipient of serv-
> ices. (p.129)

Similarly, Ellis (1993), in recognising that professionalism can weigh heavily
in assessment practice, points out that unless front line practitioners control
the key contingencies of time and other resources 'their energies are more
consistently directed towards ensuring their own survival than advocating
on behalf of users and carers' (p.39). The nature of the 'new assessment'
practices, seen as pivotal to the implementation of the reforms, emphasize
the importance of reassessment, monitoring and review. These processes,
while vital to ensuring that valuable and scarce resources are not used
wastefully will nevertheless mean that after a review/reassessment visit
services may be withdrawn if they are deemed by professionals to be no
longer necessary. This power to provide and to take away provision ensures
that the real power in community care rests in the hands of service providers
and not users.

Many special interest and disability rights groups favour user-led assessments (although they may not be suitable for all individuals, e.g. those with
dementia). However, new assessment forms developed as a result of the
White Paper reforms, in their efforts to 'cover all the angles' and satisfy all
parties involved have become long and complex (Baldock 1993). Baldock,
citing Dant and Gearing (1990) and Harrison and Thistlewaite (1993) argues
that this process has led to them being left unused or only partially filled in.
He states: 'Instead of becoming an aid to discovering users' needs, they have
become a bureaucratic obstacle to the process' (Baldock 1993, p.7).

This can be seen as an example of the outcome of the conflict between
the notion of user-led participative services and the managerialist methods
through which such services are expected to be organized and delivered.
The existence of such conflicts is unsurprising when seen in the light of
policy which can itself be seen as paradoxical and contradictory. For instance, on the one hand, in official guidance documentation, user involvement is espoused: 'Care management makes the needs and wishes of users
and carers central to the caring process' (SSI/SWSG 1991, p.14) and 'So long
as they are competent, the users views should carry the most weight' (p.53).

On the other hand, the guidance goes on to say: 'Ultimately, however,
having weighed the views of all parties...the assessing practitioner is responsible for defining the user's needs' (p.53) and '...to enable them to

achieve, maintain and restore an acceptable level of social independence, or quality of life as defined by the particular agency or authority' (p.12).

Such contradictions may be summed up by saying that whilst needs-led assessment and user participation and choice are the ideals of community care, the extent to which they are achievable will continue to be constrained by the professional's view of what is realistically possible within limited resources. The definitions of need and acceptable quality of life may then be cut according to the available cloth.

The health service which has always had a more authoritarian 'doctor's orders' approach to care than the social services may find it particularly difficult to adapt to a stronger user voice in assessment and provision. In this regard, Gomm *et al.* (1993) argue that health service professionals in particular find the notion of users defining their own needs as difficult to accept, and as a result 'either ignore the prescribed assessment procedures, or treat them as marginal' (p.108).

Kenny (1990) points out the historical nature of professional power in the health service. He argues that professionals working from a position of power and knowledge have traditionally been perceived to have the right of defining both needs and appropriate responses. Kenny goes on to note that the responses made have had more to do with ensuring professionals' integrity and security of tenure than meeting the requirements of the consumer. Similarly, Ellis (1993) argues that much of the damaging behaviour of front line professionals can be traced to their sense of despair in trying to meet service ideals within a regime of tightly managed resources. Organizational disincentives for overspending outweigh the incentives for professionals to acknowledge users' and carers' needs which cannot be met. Ellis contends that this is dealt with by professionals covertly managing such tensions during assessment by withholding information or ensuring that the focus of the assessment remains upon aspects of care over which the practitioner has some control – even if this is not the priority or area of interest of the user.

Multi-Disciplinary Working and Assessment

Dalley (1991) points out that in proposing solutions to the problems of community care which rely heavily on collaboration between professions and services and transfers of resources between agencies and redefinition of organizational relationships, policy makers are in danger of ignoring the significance of the role that professionals within collaborating agencies may have in contributing to the success or failure of the policies. She contends that the introduction of policy measures which fail to take into account professionals' views 'in a context already marked by failure' is likely to engender further resistance and 'existing tribal ties' may provoke strong opposition. Dalley concludes that: 'Collaboration between professionals among whom there is little ideological consensus may be as hard to achieve in the future as it has proved in the past' (p.178–9). This contention needs to be seen in the context of the policy driving the community care reforms. The Policy Guidance states:

> The interface between health and social care is a key area in planning, assessment, care management, commissioning and service delivery...the objective must be to provide a service in which the boundaries between primary health care, secondary health care and social care do not form barriers seen from the perspective of the service user. (Department of Health 1990, pp.4–5)

However, as Lloyd (1991) has pointed out, although statutory agencies may be presumed to have a common interest and ideology, interdepartmental rivalry is rife. Lloyd characterizes each department as having its own way of seeing a problem, its own practised remedies and fears about the expansionist designs of others over its own closely guarded territory. He concludes that: 'collaborative partnership may well prove to be an unattainable ideal' (p.129).

Hunter (1988) argues that seeing co-ordinated service provision as the remedy for the ills of fragmentation and division is predicated on a rational model of planning which makes no allowance for: '...the multiple, and sometimes conflicting objectives of agencies, services and professionals who do not share a unitary perspective on service issues or the needs of clients' (p.171). Hunter maintains that it is misleading to consider 'frontier' problems as organizational in design and therefore resolvable by structural means. Policies presupposing effective multi-disciplinary working and collaboration as a foundation for their success assume that skills to ensure co-ordinated approaches are present and require only the appropriate structural conditions to flourish. This also makes little allowance for intra-service malfunctions which could constrain inter-service collaboration.

Dowson (1991) criticizes the 'apparent ingenuity of services in finding ways to misuse good ideas' (p.12). He argues that the reluctance of professionals to hand over power accounts for many of the problems in community care and concludes that ways of working required for its realization are inevitably corrupted by the dominant culture of services (my emphasis).

A further factor, of which little account has been taken with regard to government exhortations for agencies to work together, is the fact that budgets (health/social) are often organized in such a way as to make competition more likely than co-operation. Even before the publication of the White Paper, co-ordinated service provision had become standard rhetoric although it proved slow and difficult to achieve in practice as the poor progress of joint planning and finance systems show (Wistow 1982; Booth 1983; Hunter and Wistow 1987).

Wistow (1990) suggests that the conflicting pressures of professional imperialism and cost-shunting mean that clarification of the responsibilities of health and local authorities will be far from straightforward. He argues

that the boundaries are neither clear nor fixed with regard to what constitutes 'health care' and 'social care'. The new 'market place' view of community care, emphasising competition, can also be seen as being contradictory
in the light of exhortation for greater collaboration and joint working. The
Social Services Select Committee (1990), acknowledging the introduction of
competition in community care, went on to say:

> ...without the assurance that sufficient resources will be available to
> meet the demands of the new policies, both health and local authorities
> will have incentives to distinguish rigidly between 'health' and 'social'
> care needs. This may lead them to seek to assign responsibility for
> providing services to the other agency rather than, as is necessary,
> working together to provide the best possible services needed by
> vulnerable people living in the community. (House of Commons 1990,
> para. 93)

Wistow (1990) suggests that whilst local authorities are now seen as having
the lead role for 'community care' as a whole, this is not entirely the case.
Rather, they are responsible only for the 'social care' element of it and health
authorities remain responsible for all those elements of community care that
they provide.

It is clear that uncertainties about social/health care boundaries and
responsibilities persist. There are also indications (Caldock 1993) that different groups of health professionals may be unwilling to accept the assessment
and recommendations of non-medically qualified workers (social workers,
home care organisers) as sufficient to act upon. Reassessment by professional
groups 'seeing for themselves' would effectively undermine the envisaged
benefit of a single care/case manager being responsible for planning and
implementing a care package.

At the inter-professional level, similar difficulties with shared language
and meaning are apparent and such difficulties are to be found not only
between professional groups, but also between professionals and lay people,
who tend to look at situations with a different logic (Twigg and Atkin 1994).
As Ellis (1993) has argued, this is carried over into the assessment process,
which is often rooted in the professional identity of the assessor and thereby
limited as a consequence. This might be less problematic if different professional groups all applied the same logic, but such is rarely the case. The
primary responsibility of community care now rests firmly with social
services and care managers are most often drawn from this agency. It is likely,
therefore, that much work will be needed to overcome assessment practices
and service provisions that remain driven largely by professional identity.
Such assessments would tend to invite criticism and lack of agreement by
other professional groupings in putting a care package together.

Discussion: Whither Assessment?

It is clear that practitioners need to shed narrow professional perspectives if they are to move towards the ideal of holistic and needs-led assessments. However, working against this dynamic towards individualized holistic assessments, it has been argued (Stalker 1992) that care management is changing the value-base of social work and replacing the therapeutic relationship by standardized assessments and practical problem-solving. Middleton (1994), in criticizing the post-White Paper development of new assessment proformas argues that there is a confusion between the need to collect standardized information for the day-to-day delivery of services and individualized assessment. She reserves particular criticism for 'tick box' systems of assessment, describing them as a collection of 'near misses'. A measure of a good assessment process in Middleton's view is how well it operates as a decision-making process and not on the quantity of information collected.

More generally, Fisher (1989) has argued that the account of care management given in the White Paper is 'so lacking in practice content, it can hardly be described as a technique' (p.211). The same can probably be said of assessment, and if the policy and guidance documents are long on rhetoric they are remarkably short on specifics and attempts to advance a clear conceptual framework for assessment with agreed and consistent definitions. There is no widely accepted definition of care management either (Huxley 1993) and, along with assessment, the implementation of policy in these areas has depended greatly on the systems and procedures developed at local level.

It is, perhaps, the lack of clear and agreed definitions and frameworks for assessment within and between agencies that poses the greatest challenge to the success of community care as it is envisaged in the White Paper. Until practitioners have a basis for agreement about what it is they are assessing, what the priorities are, and how the needs of an individual may best be met within a broad range of options, it is hard to see how effective care management can follow. Narrowly focused or professionally biased assessments are likely to lead to inappropriate, ineffective and, at worst, dependency-producing interventions.

Despite the continued exhortation for agencies to 'work closely together', recent evidence suggests that lines of communication between health and social services remain poor (Lloyd 1991; Allen et al. 1992; Ellis 1993) and even where care management practices are established, collaboration between agencies may be variable and multi-disciplinary working not greatly in evidence (Stalker 1992). It can be argued that whilst the White Paper addressed a number of important problems that have beset community care over the last two or three decades, it failed to address the most fundamental issues of the conceptualization, definition and practice of assessment and care management. Whilst these remain unclear and the subject of inter-professional rivalry and disagreement, divisions are likely to persist and difficulty be encountered in implementing lasting joint working practices (the acid test often seems to be how long new working arrangements continue when novelty or 'special project' status has worn off).

The situation with regard to new market-style and competitive budgeting and working will also need close monitoring in order to assess the impact on collaborative working styles. It may well prove that in an environment of retrenchment and tightly controlled resources front-line practitioners may find themselves under pressure to more tightly define boundaries and reject tasks that may lie in the grey areas between services. This would achieve the very opposite of the blurring of boundaries envisaged in the White Paper.

Research evidence suggests that the extensive history of service fragmentation and division between health and social services can be overcome (Challis and Davies 1986). Whilst care management is not a panacea for the ills of community care, it nevertheless represents our best chance of creating the ideal of a 'seamless service'. However, in defining the ideal end goal of a seamless service, it seems that policy makers have failed adequately to recognize that to build towards end goals certain foundation stones must first be in place. These include: clear and shared definitions and understandings about terms such as assessment and care management and the recognition that it will take more than regular exhortations for agencies to work together effectively to make it happen. Policy makers may find that they have set in place new market-style processes in community care that lead to competition and the very opposite effect of blurred boundaries. For progress from holistic multi-disciplinary assessment to the smooth functioning of care management to become feasible, joint training is an immediate need, but in the longer term, it may only be joint funding that finally achieves a bridging of divisions sufficient to make effective community care a reality.

References

Allen, I., Hogg, D. and Peace, S. (1992) *Elderly People: Choice, Participation and Satisfaction*. London: Policy Studies Institute Publishing.

Baldock, J. (1993) 'Participation in home based care.' *Innovation and Participation in Care of the Elderly*. Italy meets Europe, International Conference: Rome, May 20–22nd 1993.

Baldwin, S. (1986) 'Problems with needs – where theory meets practice.' *Disability, Handicap and Society 2*, 1, 41–59.

Beardshaw V. and Towell, D. (1990) *Assessment and Case Management: Implications for the Implementation of 'Caring for People.'* Briefing Paper 10. London: King's Fund Institute.

Booth, T. (1983) 'Collaboration and the social division of planning.' In Research Highlights No 7, *Collaboration and Conflict: Working With Others*. University of Aberdeen: Dept. of Social Work.

Caldock, K. (1992) *Not a Positive Choice: Elderly People Under Pressure to Enter Residential Care.* University of Wales: Bangor, CSPRD Working Paper.

Caldock, K. (1993) 'A preliminary study of changes in assessment: examining the relationship between recent policy and practitioners' knowledge, opinions and practice.' *Health and Social Care 1*, 3, 139–146.

Caldock, K. and Nolan, M. (1994) 'Assessment and community care: are the reforms working?' *Generations Review: Journal of the British Society of Gerontology 4*, 3, Nov 1994.

Challis, D. and Davies, B.P. (1986) *Case Management in Social and Health Care.* Canterbury: PSSRU, University of Kent at Canterbury.

Dalley, G. (1991) 'Beliefs and behaviour: professionals and the policy process. *Journal of Aging Studies 5*, 2, 163–180.

Dant, T. and Gearing, B. (1990) 'Keyworkers for elderly people in the community: case managers and care co-ordinators.' *Journal of Social Policy 19*, 3. 331–60.

Department of Health (1989) *Caring for People: Community Care in the Next Decade and Beyond.* (Cmnd 849). London: HMSO.

Department of Health (1990) *Caring for People: Community Care in the Next Decade and Beyond: Policy Guidance.* London: HMSO.

DHSS (1985) *Supplementary Benefit and Residential Care: Report of a Joint Central and Local Government Working Party.* London: DHSS.

Dingwall, R., Eekelaar, J.M. and Murray, T. (1983) *The Protection of Children:State Intervention and Family Life.* Oxford: Blackwell.

Dowson, S. (1991) *Moving To The Dance: Service Cultures and Community Care.* London: Values into Action.

Ellis, K. (1993) *Squaring the Circle: User and Carer Participation in Needs Assessment and Community Care.* University of Birmingham: Joseph Rowntree Foundation.

Fisher, M. (1989) *Client Studies.* Sheffield: JUSSR.

Gomm, R., Cathless-Hagen, A., Rudge, D. and Smith, R. (1993) 'Whose need is it anyway? a care management project in Cheltenham.' In R. Smith, L. Harrison, L. Gaster, R. Means, L. Martin and P. Thistlewaite (eds) *Working Together for Better Community Care.* Bristol: SAUS Publications.

House of Commons (1990) *Select Committee on Community Care.* London: HMSO.

Hudson, B. (1992) 'Ignorance and apathy.' *Health Service Journal*, 19 March 1992, 24–25.

Hunter, D. and Wistow, G. (1987) *Community Care in Britain: Variations on a Theme.* London: King Edward's Hospital Fund for London.

Hunter, D. (1988) 'Meeting the challenge of coordinated service delivery.' In B. Gearing, M. Johnson and T. Heller (eds) *Mental Health Problems in Old Age.* Chichester: J. Wiley and Sons.

Hunter, D. and Wistow, G. (1991) *Elderly People's Integrated Care System (EPICS): An Organisational, Policy and Practice Review*, Nuffield Institute Report No.3. Leeds: Nuffield Institute for Health.

Huxley, P. (1993) 'Case management and care management in community care.' *British Journal of Social Work 23*, 4, 365–82.

Kenny, T. (1990) 'Community care: a health policy dilemma.' *Senior Nurse 10*, 5, May 1990, 23–27.

Lloyd, P. (1991) 'The empowerment of elderly people.' *Journal of Aging Studies 5*, 2, 125–135.

Mayer, J. And Timms, N. (1970) *The Client Speaks: Working Class Impressions of Casework*. London: Routledge and Kegan Paul.

Middleton, L. (1994) 'Little boxes are not enough.' *Care Weekly*, 20th Jan 1994.

Lieberman, M.A. (1974) 'Symposium – long-term care: research, policy and practice.' *The Gerontologist 14*, 6, Dec 1974.

Nolan, M. and Grant, G. (1992) *Regular Respite: An Evaluation of a Hospital Rota Bed Scheme for Elderly People*. London: Age Concern Institute of Gerontology, Research paper no 6.

Norman, A. (1980) *Rights and Risk: A Discussion Document on Civil Liberty in Old Age*. London: National Corporation for the Care of Old People (NCCOP), Regents Park.

Poyner, B. and Hughes, N. (1978) *A Classification of Fatal Home Accidents*. London: The Tavistock Institute of Human Relations. 2T140. (Report to the Department of Prices and Consumer Protection).

Rowbottom, J. (1992) *Seamless Service – A Stitch in Time: Care in the Community*. London: Occasional paper No.1, Institute of Health Services Management.

Sainsbury, E. (1980) 'Client need, social work method and agency function: a research perspective.' *Social Work Service 23*, 9–15.

Seebohm Report (1968) *Report of the Committee on Local Authority and Allied Personal Social Services*. London: HMSO.

Sinclair, I. and Williams, J. (1990) 'Domiciliary services.' In I. Sinclair, R. Parker, D. Leat and J. Williams. *The Kaleidoscope of Care: A Review of Research on Welfare Provision for Elderly People*. London: NISW, HMSO.

Social Services Committee (1990) Session 1989–90, Fifth report, Community Care: Carers. London: House of Commons, HMSO.

Social Work Services Inspectorate/Scottish Office Social Work Service Group (1991) *Care Management Assessment: Practitioners Guide*. London: HMSO

Stacey, M. (1988) *The Sociology of Health and Healing: A Textbook*. London: Unwin Hyman.

Stalker, K. (1992) *Tayside Community Care Pilot Projects: Evaluation of Assessment Proformas*. Report to Tayside Regional Council, Social Work Research Centre, University of Stirling.

Twigg, J. and Atkin, K. (1994) *Carers Perceived: Policy and Practice in Informal Care*. Buckingham: Open University Press.

Wilkin, D. and Hughes, B. (1986) 'The elderly and the health service.' In C. Phillipson and A. Walker (eds) *Ageing and Social Policy: A Critical Assessment*. Aldershot: Gower.

Wistow, G. (1982) 'Collaboration between health and local authorities: why is it necessary?' *Social Policy and Administration 16*, 1, 44–62.

Wistow, G. (1990) *Community Care Planning: A Review of Past Experiences and Future Imperatives*. London: Department of Health.

CHAPTER 4

Needs-Led Assessment
The Practitioner's Perspective

Christine Futter and Bridget Penhale

Introduction

One of the inherent and fundamental principles of the National Health Service and Community Care Act, 1990, (referred to hereafter as the 1990 Act) is that of needs-led assessment of individuals who appear to be in need of community care services. In this chapter, an overview of the assumptions which underpin the concept will be examined, primarily through a review of the literature. Five main themes which can be identified from this overview will then be discussed: individualized assessments; choice; objective analysis of need; targeting and partnership with service users and their carers. From these themes, both theory and research will be linked to case examples. The extent to which needs-led assessment is achievable in practice will be examined.

By way of conclusion, the contradictions which are apparent within both common understandings and expectations of the principle are summarized. The rhetoric of choice and independence will be shown to be severely compromised by the realities which arise due to both rationing and priority-setting which local authorities are having to undertake. Attention will also be given to the lack of concordance between the emphasis on user involvement and managerialist tendencies which arise in the assessment process. Ultimately, there are no easy and readily acceptable solutions to the difficulties encountered in trying to meet the needs of individuals when resources are finite.

Review of the Literature

The Political, Economic and Social Background

In order to gain a clear understanding of the development of the concept of needs-led assessment it is important to locate it within the context of the existing policy and legislative framework. The background legislation includes both the Disabled Person's Act (1986) and the Children Act (1989), leading to the 1990 Act. Underpinning the legislation, however, are an array of assumptions and beliefs about the nature of welfare which occur at both ends of the political spectrum. It is due to the fact that the concept of needs-led assessment is located within the wider framework of these differing political views that there is some apparent divergence in responses to the perception of the success (or otherwise) of the concept in practice. It is useful, in addition, to discuss briefly some of the political and economic pressures in order to provide an appropriate context for the concept.

Throughout the past three decades, the pressures faced by administrations of both Labour and Conservative governments have been increasing. Growth in the total public expenditure had been experienced by all western countries since the 1950s (Leat 1986) but was slowing down by the late 1970s. The relative increase in the number of economically dependent people in relation to those who were economically productive began to produce arguments about the 'burdens of dependency'. From the late 1970s, a policy of retrenchment was apparent. Crossland's famous statement 'the party's over' heralded the publication of the Labour document 'Priorities for Health and Social Services' (1976) and this was followed by the Conservative publication 'Care in Action' (DHSS, 1981). Both documents gave overt and explicit recognition to a need to identify priorities in expenditure and to manage limited resources for health and welfare within existing budgets. There was a clear statement that the expenditure on social welfare must be preceded by the adequate production of economic wealth.

From 1979, however, the economic policies of the Conservative government became more radical. These policies sought ultimately to reformulate the parameters of state responsibility and the terms on which distribution of the provision of welfare should be premised. The justification for these political concepts and assumptions were derived, principally, from such market theorists as Hayek (1960) and Friedman and Friedman (1980). The thinking of this 'new right' tapped a groundswell of concern about the efficiency and effectiveness of state welfare provision. The implications drawn from such thinking were clearly that large scale provision of welfare support (some would say monopoly based) for individuals created and fostered a culture of dependency which was anachronistic in terms of the current society where real incomes for the employed were continuing to rise. In addition to this was the appearance of broader, but not incompatible, social policies which advocated individualism: self-help and personal responsibility for actions. The speech given by Fowler in 1985 (the so-called 'Buxton Speech', McCarthy 1990) encapsulated the predominant political ethos of that time with the promotion of private and voluntary provision of care for those in need in a new 'mixed economy' of welfare. The prevailing ideology can also be seen in such statements as: 'Community care means care by the community' (DHSS 1981a).

At the same time as this shift in political and economic thought, the field of social welfare was seeing the development of concepts concerning de-institutionalization. The restrictive and de-humanizing effects of institutions (in particular those concerned with mental health) had been recognized and documented (Laing 1965; Goffman 1961). Additionally, from the early 1980s an increasing number of publications had been documenting the ineffectiveness of public sector provision of welfare (Hadley and Hatch 1981; Barclay 1982; Audit Commission 1986; Kings Fund 1987; Griffiths 1988). Such writings argued for the creation of a pluralist system of welfare.

The Wagner Report, published in 1988 added a further complexity to the field by highlighting the problems arising from public funding of private residential care and the apparent perverse incentives available to older people to enter residential care and obtain assistance with funding. From the early 1980s there had been a shift of emphasis from the traditional view that only people with means could afford to enter private care to provision by the DHSS of payments towards the cost of such care. This had resulted in a rapid increase in the number of people exercising their right to choose care and to enter private care homes; to an escalating bill for government running into millions of pounds of payments via the DHSS for care (and a need to control this) and suspicions on the part of government that the vast majority of elderly people entering private homes did not require that level of care as eligibility for DHSS assistance was based on income with no assessment of care needs. This latter view was not, however, borne out by research (see Allen, Hogg and Peace 1992, for further exposition).

These aspects were picked up again in the Griffiths report (1988) which discussed the need to assist people to remain living at home and for there to be a new system for funding of private residential care from the public purse. The development of real alternatives to institutional care was expounded, together with exhortations that government policies and state provision of welfare should move away from resource and service-led provision to needs-led provision and that individuals and their carers should be offered more choice of provision. Yet a further argument developed from the Canadian based 'service brokerage' model of case management in which a shift from the provision of standardized types of care to more individualized services was advocated. Furthermore, within such systems, client advocacy and user control of service provision was seen as the way forward (Salisbury 1989; Brandon 1989).

Community care, care management and needs-led assessment have a variety of different meanings for different people. This can be seen not just in the public/professional interface, but also at the inter-disciplinary level. To expand slightly, the political right appear to have developed the concepts to fit with the perception of low cost solutions to social problems (care in the community being seen consistently as a lower cost option than residential care). Within this type of model, the development of private forms of welfare is welcomed and the responsibility of the state for collective provision of welfare is marginalized and residualized. On the other hand, the political left has viewed such concepts as an opportunity to promote user empowerment and also to demystify the professionalization of welfare systems (and in particular, professional assessments of individuals). Although such views are polarized and have been somewhat exaggerated in order to emphasize the extent of the continuum, elements of each type of view appear in the current publications pertaining to needs-led assessment. The degree to which the ideal is achievable depends partly on the ideological and political stance of the particular author and also on their own interpretation of policy. Having looked, albeit briefly and somewhat cursorily, at the background to the development of community care concepts the next section examines five main themes which appear in the current literature.

Individualized Assessments

The White Paper of 1989 outlined the responsibilities of social services departments to assess the needs of individuals for social care and to design and implement 'packages of care' which were to be specifically tailored to those needs (para. 3.1.3). A 'proper assessment of need' (para. 1.11) was to be the main objective and the 'cornerstone of high quality care'. The actual mechanics of how this was to be achieved was much less clear; more emphasis was placed on the outcomes than the processes and relationships involved in assessments (more will be said concerning this later). The subsequent guidance documents produced by the Department of Health attempted to expand the concept and theoretical bases of needs-led assessment without clarifying in absolute terms what the actual practice might consist of. Thus, for example, in the manager's guide, are found suggestions that training for staff in anti-discriminatory practice may be one way of addressing tendencies by practitioners towards responding to need in stereotypical ways (DOH/SSI 1991a, para. 5.26).

Taylor and Devine explore the concept of need further, suggesting that needs can be defined in a somewhat more proactive manner in terms of 'what is desired, rather than what is lacking' (Taylor and Devine 1993, p.38). Differing techniques of assessment are analyzed rather more comprehensively by Smale and Tuson who propose different models of assessment to enhance both the knowledge base and the understanding of the processes involved (Smale and Tuson 1993). The models offered are: 'Questioning', 'Exchange' and 'Procedural'. Of these models, the Exchange model is viewed as more empowering for individual clients as the practitioner's role is to negotiate and make agreements with the client about their needs and the best way of meeting these. The client is viewed positively as the expert on themselves and their own needs. This links firmly to a model in which the client is seen as their own 'care manager' using the negotiating and service brokerage skills of practitioners in order to obtain services to meet their own distinctive set of needs.

There are problems, however, in terms of operationalizing this type of model. Although research demonstrates a commitment to the principle of viewing needs on an individual basis, it would appear that some practitioners limit the extent to which need is recognized within assessments (in a covert rather than an overt way) due to the pressure which they perceive to remain within tightly managed budgets (Ellis 1993; Health Committee 1993). This trend was also apparent in the reluctance of some social services departments, early on in the implementation phase of community care arrangements, to recognise the existence of 'unmet needs' of individuals, lest there be a requirement that those needs should be met.

It should be acknowledged here, however, that the individualization of need is not necessarily viewed as a positive, enabling and constructive approach for clients. Theorists whose perspective incorporates views about social oppression, for example, argue that such an approach means that need is equated with deficiency and tends to pathologize the individual. Mcknight claims '...the client is less the consumer than the raw material for servicing the system...' (Mcknight 1977, p.74). The perception of clients and their needs as 'problems' requiring resolution is held to prevent practitioners from dealing with the structural and attitudinal barriers which exist within society and which disempower individuals (Oliver 1990).

There are further potential difficulties in the persistence of a rather simplistic view of assessment as a one-off exercise. Life is not static; change is constantly occurring; assessment is a process and perhaps somewhat better understood within the context of a relationship between cared for, carer and assessor. As Parsloe and Stevenson (1993) noted:

> We were told repeatedly that such assessment, planning and action can take place only within a relationship; then there is a chance service users and carers will be empowered.

> Without a relationship the process, which is about understanding another human being, becomes an impertinent entry into another's personal world. (p.25)

Choice

Choice is, arguably, one of the central tenets of both the White Paper (1989), which was produced following the Griffiths Report, and the 1990 Act. The promotion of choice and increased independence for individuals via the provision of care by non-statutory providers was seen as a critical element of the policy. It was argued that the shift for local authority social services departments to an 'enabling' role to stimulate the development of private forms of care would result in benefits for the individual 'consumer' as services would be provided more cost effectively and would meet the needs of individuals more flexibly. The practical methods for achieving this would be addressed through the development of assessment and care management with the emphases on individual needs and the development of care packages specifically designed and implemented to meet the needs of individuals. This view reflects the consumerist perspective outlined above and is rooted in the market approach to social care with a strong emphasis on obtaining value for money.

Critics of this approach have argued strongly that choice is restricted by financial constraints which have been imposed on local authorities by government (Schorr 1992; Walker 1993). It is firmly stated that although systems of care management emphasize the importance of choice for clients, financial limitations in terms of actual budgets will inevitably mean that choice will be re-interpreted and translated into the provision of the least expensive option for care. Indeed, an early report on the implementation of community care produced by the Social Services Inspectorate concluded that choice and self-determination (of clients) were in danger of being compromised by bureaucratic methods of resource allocation which appeared to be developing (DOH/SSI 1993b).

It has also been shown by research that development of private and independent sector domiciliary services is slow and that there is great variation in terms of availability of such provision depending on geographical location. Sinclair and colleagues found services to be under developed, fragmented, diverse and heavily reliant on a part-time female work force. There was little training and supervision provided and standards varied markedly between schemes (Sinclair 1993). Cromwell notes that the cumulative effect of this is likely to be in the development of culturally insensitive services which reinforce existing patterns of institutional sexism and racism '...by faithfully replicating the traditional hierarchy of staff...' (Cromwell 1992, p.45). This echoes comments made by Jack (1992) and Phillipson (1982) particularly in relation to work with older people. In addition, there is some evidence emerging that the development of a mixed economy of social care and the promotion of the independent sector requires some fundamental changes to working practices, for example, a cessation of the practice of giving precedence to in-house services which some practitioners appear to operate (Leece 1995). There are some indications, however, that a more mixed economy of provision is beginning to develop in some areas, together with a greater range of services and support (Henwood 1995).

Furthermore, the idea of an informed user making choices in terms of service provision as envisaged in the White Paper (1989) and recommended in such documents as 'Getting the Message Across' (Neill 1991) would appear to be somewhat misguided in terms of the reality of current day practice as it has been developing since implementation of the reforms. There is evidence accumulating from recent research studies which indicates the level of difficulties experienced by clients and their carers in accessing information and of obtaining adequate assessments and services (Allen, Hogg and Peace 1992; Age Concern 1993; Marsh and Fisher 1992; Ellis 1993; Warner 1994). Recent findings also suggest that assessment may not be understood by people who are in the early stages of newly acquired dependency (for example, following strokes) and, in addition, that assessment processes should move beyond the mere provision of information and

organizational structures (Baldock and Ungerson 1995). There are also inherent tensions and contradictions between the rhetoric evident within
policy guidance emphasizing choice, partnership and participation and
assessment and care management being the province of local authorities. Is
it really possible to exercise real choice when another is assessing and
determining needs and then managing the package of care? And in any case,
choice may well be constrained by availability and other forms of rationing
in times of significant constraints on resources.

Enabling choice via needs-led assessment for disadvantaged minority
groups receives only brief attention in the White Paper (1989, para. 2.9). The
subsequent guidance issued by the Social Services Inspectorate (1992) appears to be almost as vague, optimistically suggesting that discrimination at
both personal and institutional levels should be addressed by the articulation of individual needs (via proper needs-led assessments of individuals).
The principal weakness in this argument is that it has effectively been
undermined by the pressure placed on local authorities to achieve low costs
in terms of service provision and the development of use of block contracts
by them (DOH 1990; SSI report 1993). The effect of this has been the limitation
of choice and flexibility for users. This also, not surprisingly, adversely
affects the development of culturally sensitive services for black and ethnic
minority service users (Local Government Information Unit 1991).

Objective Analysis of Need

The complexities involved in adequately defining need has given rise to an
increasing amount of literature in recent years. Section 47 of the 1990 Act
requires the local authority: '...to assess the care needs of any person who
appears to them to be in need of community care'. However, the rather more
vexed question as to how need is to be measured is not addressed. The White
Paper contains a statement that assessment of need should be '...determined
by the Local Authority...' and '...must take account of what is available and
affordable...' (para. 3.2.1.2). Although the guidance documents produced by
the Department of Health attempt to define need somewhat more explicitly,
it is also stated that need should be viewed as a 'dynamic' and 'relative'
concept, which will vary with local and national policies (Practitioner's
Guide/DOH/SSI 1991b, para. 12–14). In consequence, the aim of objective
needs-led assessment appears to be doomed from the outset, culminating in
the statement 'Ultimately, however,...the assessing practitioner is responsible for defining user's needs.' (Practitioner's Guide/DOH 1991, para. 3.35).

There have been various attempts in the past to define need. Beveridge
in the 1940s viewed need in physical terms as a rather static concept which
could therefore be met by establishing a minimum, or subsistence, level
which would meet the individual's basic needs for survival. This view has
been questioned by such commentators as Doyal who proposed that the
whole concept of need has been in some senses hi-jacked by both profession-

als and politicians who have rather forced their own views about need onto people (Doyal 1993). In an eloquent treatise on need, Doyal strongly suggests that the principal universal (and objective) needs of physical good health and individual autonomy are the essential pre-requisites for active participation in social life by individuals.

A useful approach by Kempshall contains an examination of sociological explanations of need (Kempshall 1986). The taxonomy of need developed by Bradshaw (cited in Kempshall 1986) is viewed as useful in terms of describing how need is defined by different people, but is equally viewed as providing little to explain the derivation of need. Kempshall tries to clarify the meaning of the concept by arguing that need is principally determined by the social context in which it is located and as such is therefore a socially constructed phenomenon. Thus it is the professional rather than the individual who defines and determines need. Such a view tends to lend some credence to more recent research findings that there is a gap between the practice and intention of practitioners and that it is the practitioner rather than the client who determines what the individual's needs are (Marsh and Fisher 1992; DOH 1993a).

Targeting

It has ever been the case that the resources of social services departments have always been limited and have never achieved universality in terms of provision. This has, therefore, led to the development of targeting systems as a means of rationing provision. There is an explicit statement in connection with this in the White Paper: '...in future the Government will encourage targeting of home based services to those people whose need for them is greatest' (para. 3.2.12). This is, of course, consistent with previous statements about the need to ensure that provision (of services) falls within the requirements of budgets and resources. Evidence from such organisations as Age Concern and Carer's National Association is accruing to testify that targeting is occurring in ways such as these (Age Concern 1993; Warner 1994).

Within systems adopted for needs-led assessments to be conducted, there are implications arising from approaches which include targeting. Perhaps the most crucial of these concerns the provision of preventive work. From the recent research are recurrent issues arising from practitioners concerning the time-limited and mechanistic approaches they are having to adopt towards assessments in order to get their work done (Hudson 1993; Middleton 1994). Concern has also been expressed about the potential impact on longer term work with individuals such as counselling (Caldock 1993b and this volume; Hatfield 1993; Parsloe and Stevenson 1993). A further limitation of targeting systems can be seen in a trend towards the development of improved services for a minority of individuals with very complex needs but with the continuation of service-led or reduced responses for the majority of clients who have less complicated and lower level needs (DOH 1993c; Health Committee 1993).

The development of case/care management systems as a means of effectively targeting resources has also been subject to criticism. This has occurred at the level of such systems tending to both ration demand and also in some respects to hide the amount of need in a population (Jack 1992; Phillips 1992).There is evidence from the United States, where systems of case management originally developed, that the cost effectiveness of such systems is very difficult to prove (Callahan 1989). Additionally, in this country, Davies has encountered some difficulty in attempting to demonstrate that targeting led to improved efficiency (Davies 1992, cited in Schorr 1992).

Partnership

Recognition was given in the White Paper (1989) to the ideal of working with users and their carers throughout the processes of assessment and care management. There is a somewhat tentative statement that 'where possible' assessments should include the 'active participation' of users and carers (para. 3.2.6). No mention was made as to how this was to be achieved; nor of the possibility of conflict between the needs of individuals and their carers (either real or perceived). In addition, the question of the balance of power within the assessment process was notable by it's absence. The assessment of need appears to have been viewed as an entirely neutral concept; any political connotations of the concept were not addressed within the White Paper. Within the DOH guidance documents, however, there is recognition of the inequality in the balance of power between practitioner, user and carer (DOH/ SSI 1991b). In order to try and address this a number of suggestions are made for changes in practice. These include: sharing information, provision of advocacy where necessary and provision of separate assessments for carers.

The nature of the social worker's accountability to their employer may be affected by the assessment and care management process, leading to some conflict in responsibilities for the practitioner. The practitioner should act as an advocate on behalf of the client with service providers and, on occasion, other agencies whilst at the same time acting within resource constraints and controlling the resources of their own agency (which may also be the service provider). This may result in some cognitive dissonance for the practitioner (Festinger 1957). Davies has argued that the tension generated by such conflict is the result of social workers acting within and at the same time representing the state which employs them (Davies 1985). Research by Ellis seems to confirm this tendency (Ellis 1993) whilst Lipsky has described this type of difficulty as 'defences against discretion' and 'survival mechanisms' (Lipsky 1980). Within such tendencies are seen the development of practices by which clients are managed, categorized and treated in stereotypical ways.

For an approach to be truly needs-led, it has been suggested that practitioners should be separated from systems of budgetary control (Smith 1994). If practitioners are also accountable for budgets, it is argued, they can do nothing other than continue to act as gatekeepers in the role of rationing scarce resources. An alternative view to this is that it is only when practitioners control budgets, rather than relying on others to do this for them, that they will be likely to respond in an individualized needs-led fashion rather than in a service-led way (Kennedy, personal communication).

The approach taken above is but one possible interpretation of the concept of needs-led assessment; through examination of some of the themes which are apparent in the literature it is evident that there are certain areas which have not been covered. Perhaps the most glaring omission is that of multi-disciplinary working within assessment and care management systems. The reader is urged to read the contribution by Caldock in this volume for a thorough examination of the concept; suffice it to say in this context that the absence of attention here is purely in order to limit the field of enquiry somewhat and not to deny the importance of multi-disciplinary approaches to work with older people. The difficulties of achieving effective collaborative working, in the absence of a well developed and established tradition of such work (Allsop 1991) and the presence of long-standing professional differences in terms of value systems (Rabin and Zelner 1992; Hatfield 1993) should not be minimized, however.

Practice

In the following section, the main themes which were examined in the review of the literature will be applied to case examples. By relating theory and research to these examples, it will be possible to analyse critically the extent to which needs-led assessment is achievable in practice. Although the focus of the analysis reflects the specialist nature of both authors' work with older people, a similar analysis, probably with very similar findings, could be applied to all user groups.

Six cases have been chosen; a brief outline of each case will be given. In order to protect confidentiality, they will be referred to as cases A, B, C, D, E and F.

- Case A refers to a man of 89 years who had been diagnosed as having a debilitating lung condition and arthritis. He was referred by his GP for residential care because he 'would like to be looked after now'. He received no assistance from the social services department and his only support was limited help from a 'very good' neighbour and a private gardener. Reasonably active and independent, he was still able to drive his own car.

- Case B refers to a man of 76 years who referred himself for residential care. He described himself as 'lonely and isolated'. He

had moved to sheltered accommodation following the death of his
mother, whom he had 'nursed for twenty years'.

- Case C was referred by a health visitor for support for a carer. The
  couple were in their early 80s; the carer (wife) was looking after her
  husband who had been diagnosed as having Alzheimer's Disease.
  A sitting service of two hours per day was being provided by the
  social services home care service. The husband did not accept any
  need for support; he was not aware of, or able to, understand the
  needs of his wife.

- Case D relates to a lady of 85 years who was admitted to hospital
  with acute heart failure. Previously active and independent, she
  received one visit a week from the home care service and was well
  supported by her son and his family. She was referred for a nursing
  home placement by ward staff of the hospital.

- Case E referred himself via hospital staff for possible temporary
  assistance on return home. This man was 83 years old and had
  problems in controlling his diabetes; he had been admitted to
  hospital following a fall and head injury. He had not previously
  received any assistance at home other than from 'good friends' who
  lived nearby.

- Case F concerns a lady of 92 years who spent some time in hospital
  following a fall and fractured leg and ankle. She was referred for
  assistance at home by ward staff after a neighbour who had been
  providing help indicated that she was no longer able to do so. This
  lady had always previously refused offers of help from statutory
  services.

All of these referrals were initially framed in terms of possible/probable
services required, even when initiated by the individuals concerned (cases
B and E). In the DOH guidance documents produced prior to the implementation of community care, it was noted that '…the general public has been
conditioned into a service-led approach' (DOH/SSI 1991b, para. 3.19). It was
further suggested that unless potential clients/users were educated (by
practitioners and local authorities) to the possibilities of new services to meet
individual needs then stereotyped responses in terms of assessments and
care packages would be likely to continue. As referred to earlier in this
chapter, research has begun to illuminate this problem. In particular, a report
produced by the Social Services Inspectorate concerning the implementation
of the reforms provided some evidence of service-linked procedures continuing to exist which may predetermine assessment outcomes (DOH
1993c). This trend has also been found in relation to hospital discharge of
individuals to residential and nursing homes where the outcome of an
assessment may be compromised by hospital staff discussing needs for

institutional care with a person prior to a referral to social services being made (DOH/SSI 1995).

In cases A, B and D, alternatives to residential care were discussed and explored. Both A and B's expressed wishes were to enter residential care, D desired to return home if at all possible. In case A the assessment concurred with A's view of himself as in need of care, although it appeared doubtful that he met the eligibility criteria. Further evidence to support his request for care, including his deteriorating physical and psychological state, was gathered in order to substantiate the assessment. In case B the assessment determined that the eligibility criteria for care were not met. However, what also emerged was that there was very limited knowledge of community support, or indeed of residential care. The man decided, on the basis of additional information to go to a local day care centre and to try and obtain alternative housing from a range of private and voluntary providers.

Case D differed in as much as the lady was keen to return home if at all possible and did not wish to enter any form of care. Through the course of the assessment, however, it became clear that she was not well enough physically to return home and required nursing care due to her condition. It was not possible to provide this level of care for her at home: social services departments cannot purchase nursing care for individuals in their own homes as this is a responsibility of health departments. The provision of sufficient nursing care was not forthcoming from the health department in this instance. One of the key findings from the overview of implementation of community care systems (referred to earlier) was that provision of community health care needed to be increased and improved (DOH/SSI 1993c). The lady agreed to an admission to a nursing home for a short period in order to see if her health improved sufficiently to allow her to return home; fortunately the nursing home was able to work to this care plan and a return home with a range of assistance and support eventually proved possible after several months of care and rehabilitation in the nursing home.

These case examples illustrate how the application of a purely needs-led assessment might actually deny people choice and flexibility of provision. What is being alluded to here is the equation of needs with the wants of individuals. If both A and B had been provided with residential care on the basis that this was what was being requested by them, then the opportunity for alternative choices and options might not have arisen. Equally, if the lady in case D had insisted on returning home with inadequate support it is likely that she would have been re-admitted to hospital very quickly and required permanent nursing home care (if she had survived). In case B, in particular, there was more flexibility of response; an exploration of needs which determined that residential care was not what was required or desired. Under the previous arrangements, however, it is likely that B would have been admitted to private residential care via an assessment of his financial means by the Department of Social Security (which did not assess other than financial aspects). Of course, those clients with private means to purchase their own services and care are still able to do so under current arrangements. As Schorr (1992) stated 'In short, people who had choice will continue to choose. People who have not, will not' (p.25).

These three cases also indicate the potential weight and power of the professional definition of need within assessments. Cases B and D were led, through the process of the assessment, to a re-definition of their perceptions of need; case B to a view that he did not require residential care at that point in time; case D to an acceptance that for a return home to be a realistic future option, a period of care in a nursing home was necessary. The writings of Mcknight and also of Illich suggest that the power of the professional is derived from bureaucratic decision making (Mcknight 1977; Illich 1977). Recent research also indicates that the structural and organizational constraints placed on practitioners should not be underestimated. For example, Ellis found that workers who tried to work in alliance with their clients were brought into conflict with their agencies (Ellis 1993). In order to avoid this, practitioners develop a range of coping strategies including techniques to disguise need such as failure to provide relevant information, or directing people to the cheapest services rather than those which would best meet the identified needs of the individual; in effect providing limits to user choice.

To enable people to have real choice there should be options as to the types of care and services available. In cases B, C, and E all expressed an interest in home care provided by social services. In case B, this was not provided because the need was for assistance with housework only and was deemed to be 'non-essential'. However, in case E, in a different area, this type of care was provided for a short period to assist the client to settle in at home on return from hospital. In case C, the carer would have preferred the day sitting provided by social services to be extended, rather than provision from a private agency. She expressed concern regarding the reliability and the accountability of staff from an agency, although in the event the service provided worked well. The withdrawal of basic services such as cleaning services to older people, as in case B, may have a significant effect on future demands. As Caldock has noted, the effects of changes in the home help service from domestic to personal care tasks and consequent loss of services to those people with lower-level needs requires further research (Caldock 1993a). There are also difficulties in securing adequate and consistent domiciliary services through the independent sector (either privately or by contracts via social services); this can be particularly difficult in rural areas (as indicated in the previous section with research by Sinclair 1993; Leece 1995). The confirmation of the carer's anxieties (as in case C) by such findings also serves to underline the evidence that little real choice exists for older people in terms of who or how services are provided (Allen et al. 1992).

A further problem for practitioners revolves around the lack of good quality information available for older people and their carers. Although it is a requirement for social services departments to produce information (including copies of community care plans) for the public there is some evidence that sufficient attention has not been paid to this by local authorities (DOH/SSI 1994). Access to large print copies, copies in different languages or other formats such as videotapes, cassettes, Braille or inclusion of the use of interpreters is often not available or is in very short supply. The collaborative research programme 'Good Intentions' highlighted the difficulties of encouraging choice amongst older people without access to an appropriate range of information (in terms of presentation and format) (Marsh and Fisher 1992), whilst the earlier document 'Getting the Message Across' also emphasized the need to pay sufficient attention to format and accessibility including use of language (Neill 1991).

Another major concern within practice is the effect of targeting on preventative work in general terms and more particularly with regard to counselling. In cases C, D and F the importance of establishing trust and a relationship from the outset of the assessment process was absolutely crucial to achieving effective and workable solutions. In particular, in case C, some initial counselling was necessary before the assessment proper could be completed and the care plan then devised. The significance of the practitioner's interpersonal skills was emphasized in the Practitioner's Guide (DOH/SSI 1991b). Supporting evidence for this has been accumulating from research (see Hatfield 1993; and Smale and Tuson 1993 for further exposition of this). Such research supports the contention that the provision of counselling should be viewed as an integral part of the whole process of assessment and care management and that to try and separate this from the identification of needs is a false dichotomy. Assessment is usually more than a simple 'one off' contact to determine needs; to view it as an uncomplicated and rather mechanistic task is to deny its potential (Middleton 1994). However, as indicated in the previous section, if assessment is reduced and simplified to a task to be completed as cost effectively as possible, then good practice may be confined to work of higher priority and the needs of carers for support and assistance, as in cases C and F, may well be neglected (until the law is altered to give carer's certain rights, as proposed by the Carer's National Association and passed in Parliament in July 1995).

The ideal of partnership and full participation between users, carers and practitioners is not without difficulty in terms of how it is operationalized. As has been emphasized elsewhere (Parsloe and Stevenson 1993; Walker 1993) the attitudes of practitioners to power and power-sharing are fundamental here. Indeed, recent findings indicate the continuance of power imbalance in all aspects of the relationship between user and providers, including practitioners (Henwood 1995). In all of the cases described above, genuine attempts were made by both practitioners to involve users and their carers as fully as possible. This included giving copies of the completed assessment to the individuals concerned and where differences in views occurred, these were recorded on the forms. Additionally, copies of the care plans, detailing differing levels of service provision were also provided, as were copies of the complaints leaflet with an explanation as to the procedure. Encouragement, to enable participation, was given where necessary.

However, this level of practice is not without criticism and is seen by some as rather tokenistic and paternalistic (Smith 1994) and only a first step towards the full involvement of users. The Social Services Inspectorate report on monitoring implementation of community care suggested that the development of self-assessment forms would be an appropriate (and innovative) way of achieving a needs-led approach in practice (DOH/SSI 1993c). Acknowledgement was given, however, to the fact that this might not be applicable for all user groups, for example those older people who are cognitively impaired. A further extension to this suggestion, however, is the proposal that until users can control their own resources then practice will undoubtedly be agency-led. As a consequence, it has been suggested that further research into the provision of direct cash payments to enable users to purchase their own care (extending the service brokerage model of care management) should be undertaken (BASW 1992; Health Committee 1993). This has been taken forward in a limited way by government.

Finally, carers should be as involved as possible in the assessment, and where conflicts exist, a separate assessment offered. This was particularly evident in case C, but also, to an extent, case F, where the client was unaware that the carer had reached the limit of her capabilities prior to the assessment being conducted. Even with an explicit approach by both practitioners to promote this within their practice, there is, at present, no statutory duty to provide this, nor are there rights or entitlements for carers to services such as respite care (this may be a difficult area in any case, as it may be that the user does not recognise the carer's need for respite). As stated earlier, however, this situation is likely to be rectified now that the Private Member's Bill promoted by Malcolm Wicks MP (The Carer's Recognition and Services Bill) has been successful in the first stages of it's passage through Parliament. The new legislation gives carers the right to a separate and individualized assessment. It may not necessarily result in any entitlement (of carers) to services however.

With the major emphasis of recent social policy towards care in the community effectively being care provided by the family, and, in particular, by women, great stress is placed on relatives to cope with the needs of their dependants. The effects of caring on relationships has been well documented in recent years (Levin, Sinclair and Gorbach 1989; Qureshi and Walker 1989; Audit Commission 1992; Mui and Morrow-Howell 1993). Unless respite care becomes an entitlement, as proposed in the British Medical Association's document (BMA 1993) and the research studies commissioned by the Carer's National Association (Warner 1994) and Royal College of Nursing/Spastics Society (RCN/Spastics Society 1993) then a system which is predicated on a needs-led approach is likely to have little meaning or relevance for carers.

Conclusion

The shift from a service-led to a needs-led response by practitioners is based on a requirement for both an attitudinal and cultural change in perception and practice and adequate funding at an organizational level. The extent to which users and carers will have greater choice, flexibility and control in meeting their needs will be largely dependent on these two factors. Even where local authorities are committed to the principle of needs-led assessments and responses, sufficient funding remains an essential prerequisite. From the latter part of 1994, concerns about local authorities running out of money were being raised and the Department of Health recognised the problems faced by authorities trying to meet needs within available resources. The result of budgetary limitations on the definition of needs in terms of the resultant service provision has been well documented (Allen *et al.* 1992; Cromwell 1992; Ellis 1993; Smith 1994). As has been indicated, there are very real practical problems in trying to operate a needs-led service within the established framework of resource restraint (Henwood 1995). As Phillips has summarized:

> In an ideal world assessment should be 'needs-led'; i.e. with an objective analysis of need and a presentation of the options for meeting them regardless of cost or value for money. Although community care legislation highlights the importance of needs-led assessment, in reality, rationing and prioritising, given available resources, will automatically lead to reinforcing a 'service-led' response. (Phillips 1992, p.12)

Similarly, the optimism expressed prior to the implementation of community care for greater participation by users and their carers in both assessments and in the decision-making process as a whole has proved to be limited by organizational constraints, in particular those structures concerning service provision and delivery. Care management and assessment processes appear to be developing predominantly as managerial systems concerned with the cost-effective administration of resources. The inherent conflict between the notion of user-led participation in assessment and service delivery and managerially and procedurally-(process) driven approaches creates tension and confusion for practitioners, as evidenced in the examples provided from recent practice. The idea that clients or 'customers' are to be managed is clearly at odds with the aim of empowering users and enhancing independence and casts users in the role of dependent and passive recipients of beneficent services.

As Walker has suggested, unless users and their carers are genuinely enabled to participate in the decision-making process, their power to affect the outcome of the assessment and the definition of need will continue to be marginalized (Walker 1993). Existing levels of discrimination will surely continue unless there is a change to a more qualitative, user-focused and user-led approach to the definition of need (from the current quantitative, managerial and bureaucratically based approach). Undoubtedly this type of approach will necessitate additional resource provision and allocation if it is to work effectively. It will also require a shift by practitioners to an equitable sharing of power, if not a wholesale redistribution of power to users and their carers. Such issues need to be addressed as a matter of some urgency if the very concept of community care is to stand any chance of survival let alone positive development.

References

Age Concern (1993) *No Time to Lose: First Impressions of the Community Care Reforms.* London: Age Concern.

Allen, I. (1991) (ed) *Health and Social Services: The New Relationship.* London: Policy Studies Institute.

Allen, I., Hogg, D. and Peace, S. (1992) *Elderly People: Choice, Participation and Satisfaction.* London, Policy Studies Institute.

Allsop, J. (1991) 'Primary health care: the implications of recent changes.' In I. Allen. *Health and Social Services: The New Relationship.* London: Policy Studies Institute.

Audit Commission (1986) *Making A Reality of Community Care.* London: Policy Studies Institute.

Audit Commission (1992) *The Community Revolution.* London: HMSO.

Baldock, J. and Ungerson, C. (1995) *Becoming Consumers of Community Care: Households Within the Mixed Economy of Welfare.* York: Joseph Rowntree Foundation.

Barclay Report (1982) *Social Workers: Their Role and Tasks.* London: NISW, Bedford Square Press.

Bornat, J., Pereira, C., Pilgrim, D. and Williams, F. (1993) (eds) *Community Care: A Reader.* London: Macmillan.

Brandon, D. (1989) 'Who sets the boundaries of control?' *Service Brokerage 1,* 3, Oct 1989.

British Association Of Social Workers (BASW) (1992) *A User Led Service.* Unpublished paper/discussion document. (16.3.92).

British Medical Association (BMA) (1993) *National Standards in Community Care: Targets for Provision.* London: B.M.A.

Caldock, K. (1993a) 'Service histories of elderly people.' In D. Robbins (1993) (ed) *Community Care: Findings from Department of Health Funded Research 1988–1992.* London: HMSO.

Caldock, K. (1993b) 'Assessment and care packaging after the white paper.' In D. Robbins (1993) (ed) *Community Care: Findings from Department of Health Funded Research 1988–1992.* London: HMSO.

Callahan, J.J. (1989) 'Case management for the elderly: a panacea?' *Journal of Ageing and Social Policy 1,* 1/2, 181–189.

Cromwell, N. (1992/1993) 'Assessment and accountability in community care.' *Critical Social Policy 36,* 12, 3, 40–52.

The views of the authors are their own and not those of their organization.

Davies, B. (1992) cited in A.L. Schorr (1992) *The Personal Social Services: An Outside View*. York: Joseph Rowntree Fund.

Davies, M. (1985) *The Essential Social Worker: A Guide to Positive Practice*. Aldershot: Gower.

Department Of Health (1989) *Caring for People: Community Care in the Next Decade and Beyond.*, Cmnd 849, London: HMSO.

Department Of Health (1990) *Community Care in the Next Decade and Beyond, Policy Guidance*. London: DoH, HMSO.

Department Of Health (1991) *Assessment Systems and Community Care*. Lancs: Social Services Inspectorate (SSI).

Department Of Health (1993a) *Implementing Community Care: Feedback on the Purchaser and Provider Workshops*. Lancs: Health Promotions Unit (HPU).

Department Of Health (1993b) *Monitoring and Developing: First Impressions*. Lancs: HPU.

Department of Health/Social Services Inspectorate (1991b) *Care Management and Assessment: Manager's Guide*. Milton Keynes: HMSO.

Department of Health/Social Services Inspectorate (1991b) *Care Management and Assessment: Practitioner's Guide*. Milton Keynes: HMSO.

Department Of Health/SSI (1993c) *Regional Summaries: Fifth Report on the Implementation of Caring for People*. Lancs: SSI.

Department Of Health/SSI (1993d) *Inspection of Assessment and Care Management Arrangements in Social Services Departments. Interim Overview Report, December 1993*. London: HMSO.

Department Of Health/SSI (1994) *Inspection of Assessment and Care Management in Social Services Departments October 1993-March 1994. Second Overview Report*. London: HMSO.

Department Of Health (1995) *Moving On: Report of the National Inspection of Social Services Department Arrangements for the Discharge of Older People from Hospital to Residential or Nursing Home Care*. London: HMSO.

Department of Health and Social Security (DHSS) (1976) *Priorities for Health and Personal Social Services in England*. London: HMSO.

DHSS (1981) *Care in Action*. London: HMSO.

DHSS (1981a) *Care in the Community*. London; HMSO.

Doyal, L. (1993) 'Human need and the moral right to optimal community care.' In J. Bornat, Pereira, C., Pilgrim, D. and Williams, F. (1993) (eds) *Community Care: A Reader*. London: Macmillan.

Ellis, K. (1993) *Squaring the Circle: User and Carer Participation in Needs Assessment*. Birmingham: University of Birmingham/Joseph Rowntree Foundation.

Festinger, L. (1957) *A Theory of Cognitive Dissonance*. Stanford Ca: University of Stanford Press.

Friedman, M. and Friedman, R. (1980) *Free to Choose*. London: Macmillan.

Goffman, E. (1961) *Asylums*. New York: Doubleday.

Griffiths, Sir R. (1988) *Community Care: Agenda for Action*. London: HMSO.

Hadley, R. and Hatch, S. (1981) *Social Welfare and the Failure of the State*. London: George Allen and Unwin,

Hatfield, B. (1993) 'Support services for people with disabilities: some lessons for care management.' *Health and Social Care in the Community* 1, 6, 365–372.

Hayek, F.A. (1960) *The Constitution of Liberty.* London: Routledge and Kegan Paul.

Health Committee (1993) *Community Care: The Way Forward.* London: HMSO.

Henwood, M. (1995) *Making a Difference?: Implementation of the Community Care Reforms Two Years On.* London: King's Fund Centre.

Hudson, H. (1993) 'Needs-led assessment: nice idea, shame about the reality?' *Health and Social Care in the Community* 1, 2, 115–116.

Illich, I. (1977) (ed) *Disabling Professions.* London: Marion Boyars.

Jack, R. (1992) 'Case management and social services: welfare or trade fair?' *Generations Review* 2, 1, 4–7, March 1992.

Kempshall, H. (1986) *Defining Client's Needs in Social Work.* Social Work Monographs, Norwich: UEA.

King's Fund (1987) *Facilitating Innovation in Community Care.* London: King's Fund.

Laing, R. (1965) *The Divided Self: An Existential Study in Sanity and Madness.* Harmondsworth: Penguin.

Leat, D. (1986) 'Privatisation and voluntarisation.' *Quarterly Journal of Social Affairs* 2, 3, 290–291.

Leece, J. (1995) 'Professional's attitudes and the mixed economy: implementing community care in Cheshire.' *Elders* 4, 1, 5–16.

Levin, E., Sinclair, I. and Gorbach, P. (1989) *Families, Services and Confusion in Old Age.* Aldershot: Avebury.

Lipsky, M. (1980) *Street Level Bureaucrats.* New York: Russell Sage.

Local Government Information Unit (1991) *Community Care Comment: The Black Community and Community Care.* London: Wernham Printers Ltd.

Marsh, P. and Fisher, M. (1992) *Good Intentions: Developing Partnership in Social Services.* York: Joseph Rowntree Foundation.

McCarthy, M. (1990) *The New Politics of Welfare.* London: Macmillan.

Mcknight, J. (1977) 'Professionalised service and disabling help.' In I. Illich (ed) *Disabling Professions.* London: Marion Boyars.

Middleton, L. (1994) 'Little boxes are not enough.' *Care Weekly,* 20th January 1994.

Mui, A.C. and Morrow-Howell, N. (1993) 'Sources of emotional strain among the oldest caregivers.' *Research on Aging* 15, 1, 50–69.

Neill, J. (1991) *Getting the Message Across: A Guide to Developing and Communicating Policies, Principles and Procedures on Assessments.* London: HMSO.

Oliver, M. (1990) *The Politics of Disablement.* London: Macmillan.

Parsloe, P. and Stevenson, O. (1993) A powerhouse for change. *Community Care* 2 March 1993, 24–25.

Phillips, J. (1992) 'The future of social work with older people.' *Generations Review* 2, 4, December, 1992, 12–14.

Phillipson, C. (1982) *Capitalism and the Construction of Old Age.* London: Macmillan.

Qureshi, H. and Walker, A. (1989) *The Caring Relationship.* London: Macmillan.

Rabin, C. and Zelner, D. (1992) 'The role of assertiveness in clarifying roles and strengthening job satisfaction of social workers in multi-disciplinary mental health settings.' *British Journal of Social Work* 22, 1, 17–32.

Royal College Of Nurses And Spastics Society (1993) *Day In, Day out: A Survey of Views of Respite Care.* London: RCN.

Salisbury, B. (1989) 'Towards dignity and self-determination.' In *Service Brokerage 1,* 3, October, vi–vi.

Schorr, A.L. (1992) *The Personal Social Services: An Outside View.* York: Joseph Rowntree Foundation.

Sinclair, I. (1993) 'Literature review of community care for old people in England and Wales (EC project).' In D. Robbins (1993) (ed) *Community Care: Department of Health Funded Research 1988–1992.* London: HMSO.

Smale, G. and Tuson, G. (1993) *Empowerment, Assessment, Care Management and the Skilled Worker.* London: HMSO.

Smith, J. (1994) 'Shopping for the right stuff.' *Care Weekly 10,* 94, p.9.

Taylor, B. and Devine, T. (1993) *Assessing Needs and Planning Care in Social Work.* Hants: Ashgate Publishing, Ltd.

Wagner Report (1988) *Residential Care: A Positive Choice.* London: HMSO.

Walker, A. (1993) 'Community care Policy: from consensus to conflict.' In J. Bornat, Pereira, C., Pilgrim, D. and Williams, F. (1993) (eds) *Community Care: A Reader.* London: Macmillan.

Warner, N. (1994) *Community Care: Just a Fairy Tale?* London: Carer's National Association.

CHAPTER 5

On the Margins
Care Management and Dementia

Rosemary Bland

Introduction

This chapter examines the community based support of a group of individuals who were caring for elderly relatives with dementia. Drawing on an evaluation of a pilot care management project for frail elderly people in Scotland (Elderly People in the Community, EPIC) funded by the Nuffield Foundation, it discusses the difficulties carers looking after someone with dementia experienced and examines the project's outcomes. Given the disappointing results for these carers compared with what was achieved for carers of non-demented project users, some doubt is cast on the effectiveness of care management in avoiding institutionalization of people with dementia and the appropriateness of promoting long-term care at home rather than high quality institutional care for this particular group.

The Policy Background

The Audit Commission (1986) having documented the organizational and financial constraints and barriers to implementing community care successfully, the Griffiths Report (1986) and the subsequent White Paper 'Caring for People' (1990) accepted the arguments and the challenges posed. Finally, the National Health Service and Community Care Act (1990) gave local authorities the responsibility for assessing and meeting the needs of residential and community care service users.

This new legislation promoted development of domiciliary, day and respite service to enable people to live in their own homes where feasible and sensible, endorsed proper assessment of need and care management as the way to achieve this and made practical support for carers a high priority. The Act gave certain groups of adults the right to have their social care needs at least assessed by social services/work departments, if not actually met. For the first time the needs of family members, friends and neighbours providing care were also recognized both as carers and as individuals in their own right who may have social care needs of their own. Their need for support (to continue caring!) was also highlighted as a key objective of the legislative changes.

The EPIC Project

Given these policy developments and changes, the EPIC project seemed to be well timed, starting as it did shortly after 'Caring for People' was published (Department of Health 1989). It was seen as an opportunity to experiment before the legislation was implemented and to discover whether the seed of care management which had seemed to flourish in several earlier English experiments would do as well in the rather cooler climate of enthusiasm for it in Scotland, where higher populations of community care user groups (although not elderly people) still lived in long-stay hospital care. EPIC recruited staff from a mix of health and social work backgrounds which, it was hoped, would encourage and develop better interdisciplinary working to the benefit of users.

The new post of 'Home Carer' was established, akin to the multi-functional 'Community Carer' recommended by Griffiths, to provide flexible assistance at times to suit users' and carers' needs. The project had a budget to purchase services, from which these specially recruited and trained home carers were paid. The team was aware that social services had tended hitherto to be biased towards elderly people living alone and was enthusiastic to offer help to elderly people and their families in need, irrespective of their living situation. In the event, nearly two thirds (64%) of the older people referred to EPIC did live alone but many of them were also receiving considerable amounts of help from their non-resident relatives. A screening/referral form (Lutz 1989) was developed containing questions associated with high risk of social breakdown. This was used by the team to identify those elderly people and their carers in greatest need of assessment and care management (Table 5.1).

Care Management, Carers and Dementia

Earlier care management experiments in England showed very positive outcomes both for frail elderly people and their carers at lower or no greater financial costs than standard services (Challis and Davies 1986; Davies and Challis 1986; Challis et al. 1990). The first experiment in Thanet identified 24 people with some degree of confusion or disorientation, half of whom were still at home at the end of one year, as against 23 per cent in the group receiving standard social services. It is not clear how many of them were living alone and how many with carers. Compared with other people in the project, however, they proved relatively costly to support at home.

In the Gateshead study (Challis et al. 1990), 31 per cent of the 101 elderly people supported by the social care scheme and 48 per cent of the 30 elderly users supported by the health and social care scheme had a 'confusional

**Table 5.1 Ages and Lutz scores of users with
and without dementia and comparators**

	EPIC Users & Comparators		
	Users (Not Interviewed – Dementia)	Users Interviewed	Comparators
Mean Age (rounded)	83.29	82.69	82.11
Valid N	156	26	37
Cares' Mean Age	58.4	59.8	67.0
Valid N	11	22	8
Mean Lutz Score	6.17	5.62	5.17
Valid N	156	26	92

state' and 65 per cent (N=72) of the carers in the social care scheme and all of the 22 carers in the health and social care scheme were 'under stress'. This study also found confused users more expensive to maintain at home. Nevertheless, 63 per cent of social care scheme users (N=90) and 64 per cent of the health and social care project users (N=28) were still at home twelve months later, compared with just 36 per cent in the social care scheme comparator group and 21 per cent in the health and social care control group. How many of these people were confused is not clear yet the research appeared to associate carers' increased well-being with effective care management (Challis and Davies 1991).

At the end of the EPIC evaluation, the project was still supporting two older people with dementia at home, one of whom was living in sheltered housing. Four people had died, three were in long-stay hospital care and four had been admitted into residential care. In the comparator group, none of the people identified as having dementia/memory problems were still living at home at the end of the tracking period. All of them had either died or gone into long stay care. This compares with the Cambridge study of people over the age of 75 with dementia on general practice registers which found that 43 per cent of them had died by the end of the second year (O'Connor et al. 1991). In the second National Institute for Social Work study 35 per cent of older people had died just over twelve months after the first research contact and 19 per cent were in residential care but 46 per cent were still at home, being looked after by the same carer in the vast majority of cases (Levin, Moriarty and Gorbach 1994). EPIC was successful in only a very small way in keeping some of its users with dementia out of institutional care. Whether this is the appropriate outcome to aim for is one question this chapter asks rather than answers.

The EPIC care managers were aiming to support people at home for around two-thirds of the cost of long-term care. However, the care packages for people who were attending the psychogeriatric day hospital when referred were very high because that service alone was costed at £45 per day (1992 prices). Since this was a notional rather than actual cost to the project, there was no possibility of substituting cheaper service alternatives and it inflated the care package cost outside the care managers' control, leaving them little financial leeway to purchase other care for these people.

Why were these outcomes so different from the PSSRU studies which showed remarkably consistent results in three very different locations? A number of possible explanations can be advanced.

Different Patterns of Policy Development and Implementation.

Is it because Forth Valley was better provided with long-stay psychogeriatric beds than Thanet and Gateshead? As Challis has pointed out, models of care management differ and adapt according to local need and circumstance (Challis and Davies 1991). The EPIC project differed from the PSSRU schemes in several ways, not least in its lack of an 'enthusiast' or 'product champion' in either agency keen to see it succeed (Audit Commission 1986). The wholesale closure of long-stay hospital beds for elderly people in Scotland has not been as rapid as further south and many of the dementia referrals to EPIC came from a psychogeriatrician with access to long-stay hospital beds. Only very recently have local authorities and health boards had to submit joint community care plans to the Scottish Office, making previous inter-agency collaboration difficult (Titterton 1990).

The Behaviour of Clinicians

Psychogeriatricians

One psychogeriatrician was keen to obtain the services of a home carer for hard pressed relatives as soon as possible, rather than test the effectiveness of care management in retaining people with dementia at home long-term. There was, therefore, a divergence in the aims of the project and how it was used. Admission to long-stay hospital care was offered and accepted within relatively short time of people being referred to EPIC. At one stage, the project leader asked the consultant to refer only those people whose care at home could be maintained for some time as the care managers were disheartened when an elderly person with dementia was admitted to long-stay care shortly after an assessment and care plan had been implemented. This was not well received and referrals tailed off from that quarter considerably thereafter.

General Practitioners

The general practitioners of dementia sufferers were thought by carers to be slow to take further action to investigate their relative's difficulties. Some carers said they had been asking the GP for several years to have their relative's problem investigated. Care managers were quite often instrumental in getting GPs to refer patients to hospital for diagnosis but this did not mean carers were told what was wrong. From the researchers' point of view, enquiry about the nature of the elderly person's difficulties had to be made very discreetly. At first interview, only one carer had been told by the psychogeriatrician that dementia was the cause of their relative's difficulties. By the second interview, the number of carers who specifically mentioned dementia had risen to seven but only one of them had been told this by the patient's GP. Four others had learned from other sources what was wrong, including two people who recognized their relative's behaviour for what it was from seeing television documentaries about dementia. Six carers were still ignorant of their relative's condition at second interview. This failure to spell out to carers what was wrong or thought to be wrong, led to some suspicions that the elderly person was 'playing up,' 'stringing them along' or 'putting it on' when they could not remember things or behaved oddly or unpredictably. This misunderstanding caused some bad feeling between carers and the older people, to their mutual disadvantage. Relatives were encouraged by some care managers to contact the psychogeriatrician direct if they wanted to know more about their relative's difficulties but some did not do so, using lack of time as the reason; which was understandable since three of them were in full-time employment. The explanations given ranged from 'hardening of the arteries', 'memory difficulties', 'memory problems', 'very confused', to 'normal senility for her age' and 'short term memory problems' which the caring relatives themselves knew already. What they did not know was what was causing these symptoms. One spouse carer thought her husband's memory and behaviour problems were due to a hard knock on the head he had sustained as a young man and nobody disabused her of this belief.

A carer daughter in the case study sample had her mother referred for specialist diagnosis by the GP only when she herself was involved in a blood pressure research project and was found to have very high cholesterol levels, despite previous joint visits to the surgery expressing concern at her mother's deteriorating memory. It took three months to convince the blood pressure researchers that this abnormally high level was attributable not to poor diet or lack of exercise on her behalf but was possibly due to the strain of caring for her mother who had moderate to severe dementia. Only when the diagnosis of dementia had been confirmed was she put in touch with support services in EPIC.

General practitioners are often unaware of what local social services can provide and their reluctance to refer patients to departments is well established (Huntingdon 1981; Twigg 1992). This can have important repercussions for carers, since support services for them are usually provided by social services rather than health agencies. Referrals to EPIC were rarely made directly by GPs, more often by community nurses based in primary care teams, who had been monitoring the situation for some time and knew the patient well. A more recent study found that only 17 per cent of carers of elderly people interviewed had been helped by the GP to get any services specifically to help them continue to care (Allen, Hogg and Peace 1992).

Carer–Sufferer Relationship

Who cares for the elderly person and the nature of their relationship is an important factor in determining the outcome of care (Sinclair 1990; Twigg 1992; Gwyther 1989). Spouses are least likely to accept institutional care but there was only one spouse carer of an older person with dementia in the EPIC user group. The two people still at home at the end of the project had other relatives – a daughter and a sister – as their main carers. The people with dementia in our sample were physically very mobile and this resulted

Table 5.2 Gilleard Problem Checklist Scores for Problem Frequency and Seriousness at First and Second Interview

	EPIC Users & Comparators		
	Users (Not Interviewed – Dementia.)	Users Interviewed	Comparators
Mean Problem Frequency for Carer (Time 1)	28.90	16.52	–
Valid N	10	21	–
Mean Problem Frequency for Carer (Time 2)	29.11	16.87	21.63
Valid N	9	15	8
Mean Problem Seriousness for Carer (Time 1)	26.00	19.24	–
Valid N	10	21	–
Mean Problem Seriousness for Carer (Time 2)	28.67	14.14	22.99
Valid N	9	14	8

in their continual need for supervision and intervention which, given that most carers did not live with them, caused difficulties and frustrations. Table 5.2 illustrates the greater frequency and seriousness of problems identified by carers of people with dementia in the project sample. The pre-morbid relationships between some carers and elderly people, well documented as influencing outcomes in care (Gilhooly 1990), had been stormy and the illness did nothing to lessen this. Relatives expressed constant anxiety about such behaviours as wandering, accidents with fires, cookers and kettles, exploitative intruders and money going mysteriously missing.

The Degree of User Impairment

The average score on the project screening/referral form (Lutz 1989) for people with dementia was higher than that of people who were not mentally impaired and of the older people in the comparator group which had included people with dementia at the beginning of the tracking period (see Table 5.1). Although scores could have been used to prioritize project cases, this was never done as referrals were slow at first and only gradually gathered momentum as the project became better known and trusted. The people with dementia on the EPIC project were, without doubt, a group with considerable problems.

The Degree of Carer Stress

That the carers of people with dementia in the EPIC project found their role stressful was shown by their high scores on the Malaise Scale (Rutter *et al.* 1970); above the normal range and indicative of emotional stress (Table 5.3). All carers in the interviewed sample were asked about a range of behaviours in their relative and the extent to which these were problematic for them, using Gilleard's Problem Checklist (1984). Carers of the people with dementia reported many more problem behaviours at first interview than the carers of other older people and the number of problems had increased slightly by the second interview, as had their perceived severity. These carers were supporting some very demented individuals who were very difficult to sustain in the community.

Three carers lived with their older relative and were therefore more subject to the '36 hour day' (Mace and Rabins 1985), since the older person would often get up during the night when the carer had no possibility of relief. The non-resident carers were in frequent personal contact as well as by telephone, which they used to prompt their relative to carry out some specific task, such as taking medication, and as a monitoring device to keep the older person 'on the right track' between visits. For those non-resident carers, the telephone itself was sometimes the cause of broken nights, when their relative rang them in the small hours, worried about some aspect of their lives, often because they had mislaid something.

Table 5.3 Measured Carer Stress at First and Second Interview

	EPIC Users & Comparators		
	Users (Not Interviewed – Dementia)	Users Interviewed	Comparators
Mean Carer Malaise Scores (Time 1)	5.00	6.67	–
Valid N	11	18	–
Mean Carer Malaise Scores (Time 2)	5.25	4.92	5.75
Valid N	4	13	8

Changing Attitudes of Care Managers

The behaviour and changing attitudes of the EPIC care managers towards institutionalization may also have been influential over outcome. They had developed a strong sense of advocacy for users and a concern for the quality of life of both carers and the older person. Where they felt that, despite their best efforts in care planning, a move into long-stay care was ultimately unavoidable, they appeared to decide that a gradual, planned move was more in the user's interests than an emergency admission in the event of the care breaking down (through, for example, too much stress for the carer). They accordingly worked towards this end, securing day care on an increasing basis as well as respite care. Carers much appreciated this and the elderly person accepted it because the pace of change was implemented carefully. This confirms Parker's assertion that there are almost bound to be conflicts of interest between people with dementia and those who look after them (Parker 1990a). Such conflicts certainly appeared evident within the EPIC project. Gilhooly (1990), in her review of the literature on service ability to prevent institutionalization quoted several studies where increased contact with professionals and services resulted in greater, not less, likelihood of the elderly person being admitted to long-stay care (Gilhooly 1990). In their more recent study of breaks for carers of people with dementia, Levin, Mariarty and Gorbach (1994) found that those older people who had had residential relief care, as opposed to day care or a sitter service, were most likely to be in long stay residential care at follow-up. This finding was not unexpected, since this kind of support is usually targeted on the more frail and most dependent people.

Late Stage Referral

As we have said, many of the referrals of elderly people with dementia came from the day hospital in the early stages of the EPIC project. It is well documented that GPs are sometimes reluctant to refer to specialists because dementia is not yet curable and they tend only to do so when the patient is otherwise physically ill, in crisis, or their social support is likely to crumble. It seems that like a home care respite project in America (Gwyther 1989), the users with dementia were no longer on the margins of institutional care but in urgent need of it. Half of the project users were in long-stay care or dead within eight months and a quarter of them within 30 days. The author felt that the respite service was used 'often as an apparent last-ditch effort' to prolong the continuation of care at home which was the desired option (Gwyther 1989). In other words, the help afforded by the project seems generally to have been offered too late to effectively assist carers.

What did EPIC do for these Carers?

The care managers were successful in obtaining more support for the family carers. Six out of thirteen elderly people with dementia were already getting home help at the time of the first research interview. By the time of the second interview, this had risen to ten. Two of the three remaining people had help from a home carer, as did six others. The care managers were able to organize care at early and late times of day and gave the carers much needed relief not only from performing care tasks but also from the responsibility for their relative's welfare and safety, which they found very burdensome and unremitting. The first NISW Study (Levin, Sinclair and Gorbach 1989) of confused elderly people found that the principal services which were of most measurable benefit to carers were home help and respite care. For the great majority of carers in EPIC, the home help was likewise regarded very positively, as indeed were the home carers.

Other forms of support which EPIC arranged included day care in a special unit for people with dementia in a nearby residential home and respite care; episodic, to allow relatives to go on holiday and rolling, every six weeks to provide regular relief of carer strain. Once psychiatric assessment at the day hospital had been completed, people who were judged able to benefit from the social services day care were referred to the EPIC project for this to be arranged. Some elderly people disliked the day hospital and refused to go, in which case the care manager negotiated day care from the social work department for them. This resource was new and extremely flexible, offering as many days care as required over extended hours seven days a week.

The care managers themselves performed a very important personal role both for carers and the elderly people as confidante, as advocate, and as a channel of communication between all the services being provided and the families involved. This sometimes involved interpreting perceptions or wishes of individuals in a tactful way, such as explaining why someone did not wish a particular service to continue. In the second research interviews most of the carers spoke very highly indeed of the care managers saying that they could not have continued caring for their relative as long as they did without the help of the EPIC project and its workers. This is not the only study where carers have expressed genuine appreciation for help and assistance they have received but where objective measures of the burden and stressful elements of their caring responsibilities have not shown the expected and hoped-for reduction in either stress or perception of burden, nor indeed in outcome for the person with dementia.

Conclusion

Whilst some medical research pursues the cause or causes and, ultimately, the cure for the various types of dementia, other studies investigate ways of managing the course of the disease other than by hospitalization. As the Health Service pursues a policy of long-stay bed closures, dementia has been defined more and more as a 'social disease' with responsibility for the long-term support of patients viewed as more appropriately undertaken by local authorities within the context of community care. Whether the various models of care management being developed by social work/services departments are able to effectively and adequately support older people with dementia at home will depend largely on the willingness of family carers to continue their involvement. That continued willingness of carers may depend on the flexibility and sufficiency of support services and skilled care managers aware of the physical and mental costs which such commitment to people with dementia can impose.

References

Allen I., Hogg, D. and Peace, S. (1992) *Elderly People: Choice, Participation and Satisfaction*. London: Policy Studies Institute.

Audit Commission (1986) *Making a Reality of Community Care*. London: HMSO.

Challis, D. and Davies, B. (1986) *Case Management in Community Care*. Aldershot: Gower.

Challis D., Chessum, R., Chesterman, J., Luckett, R. and Traske, K. (1990) *Case Management in Social and Health Care*. Canterbury: PSSRU, University of Kent.

Davies, B. and Challis, D. (1986) *Matching Resources to Needs in Community Care*. Canterbury: PSSRU, University of Kent.

Department of Health (DOH) (1989) *Caring for People*. London: HMSO.

Gilhooly, M.L.M. (1990) 'Do services delay or prevent institutionalisation of people with dementia?' *Research Report No. 4*. Dementia Services Development Centre: University of Stirling.

Gilleard, C.J. (1984) *Living with Dementia*. London: Croom Helm.

Griffiths, Sir R. (1988) *Community Care: Agenda for Action.* London: HMSO.

Gwyther, L.P. (1989) 'Overcoming barriers: home care for dementia patients.' *Caring,* August 1989.

Huntingdon, J. (1981) *Social Work and General Medical Practice.* London: Allen and Unwin.

Levin, E., Sinclair, I. and Gorbach, P. (1989) *Families, Services and Confusion in Old Age.* Aldershot: Gower.

Levin, E., Moriarty, J. and Gorbach, P. (1994) *Better for the Break.* London: National Institute for Social Work Research Unit, HMSO.

Lutz, B. (1989) Report of Development and Testing of Screening and Assessment Instruments, Paper 12, Social Work Research Centre, University of Stirling.

Mace, N.L. and Rabins, P.V. (1985) The 36 Hour Day: Caring at Home for Confused Elderley People. London: Hodder and Stoughton in conjunction with Age Concern

O'Connor, D.W., Politt, P.A., Brook, C.P.B., Reiss, B.B. and Roth, M. (1991) 'Does early intervention reduce the number of elderly people with dementia admitted to institutions for long-term care?' *British Medical Journal 302,* 871–5

Parker, G. (1990a) 'Whose care? Whose costs? Whose benefit? A critical review of research on case management and informal care.' *Ageing and Society 10,* 459–567.

Rutter, M., Tizard, J. and Whitmore, K. (eds) (1970) *Education , Health and Behavior.* London: Longman.

Sinclair, I., Parker, R., Leat, D. and Williams, J. (1990) *The Kaleidoscope of Care: A Review of Research on Welfare Provision for Elderly People.* London: HMSO.

Titterton, M. (1990) Caring for People in Scotland: A Report on Community Care in Scotland and the Implications of the NHS and Communtiy Care Bill. Report submitted in evidence to the House of Commons Social Services Committee.

Twigg, J. (1992) *Carers: Research and Practice.* London: HMSO.

CHAPTER 6

User Choice, Care Management and People with Dementia

Mary Winner

Introduction and Background

Promoting individual choice and self determination is a core objective of assessment and care management systems as outlined in policy guidance by the Government (Department of Health 1990). This is, arguably, the most significant challenge resulting from the new thinking on community care since it questions and potentially redefines the professional role in service delivery and also gives far greater weight to users' views and preferences. The power imbalance associated with professional gatekeepers of welfare services and those seeking access to them is being seriously debated and a new understanding of this relationship beginning to emerge. The concept of partnership 'between professionals and users', has been developed by Marsh andFisher (1992) and also by Smale and Tuson (1993). Other writers, particularly in the field of disability, have gone further seeking to give even greater empowerment and control to users in both assessment and care management processes (Croft and Beresford 1990; Oliver 1990).

This evident and increased momentum towards user participation and choice does, however, appear to make certain assumptions about the consumers of welfare services. For example, it implies:

- that users know what they need and can articulate what they prefer – not only with regard to the selection of services but also in relation to their preferred lifestyle;

- that in future they will have sufficient accessible information available to enable them to make these choices about what they require;

- that they will make judgements which will advance their own self-interest and preference.

Conversely, there is also recognition that for some people it might be beneficial to use the services of an independent advocate to represent their views, or alternatively a facilitator to enable effective communication for those individuals who require assistance in this respect.

This chapter begins to tease out how the consumerist and/or needs-based approach will meet the needs of people with dementia. The estimated 500,000 older people with dementia in this country are a very significant group requiring social and personal care support. How far can this group participate about decisions regarding their welfare? What should consultation, partnership and user involvement mean for people who may have speech impairments and difficulty in communicating? How can a needs-based approach be implemented appropriately and effectively with this group of vulnerable elders?

Models of Service Delivery

At first sight there would appear to be difficulties with the new consumerist and partnership models emerging and their applicability to people with dementia. But again this depends on what assumptions are made about people with dementia. Some common assumptions are:

- that they may have difficulty in articulating needs and preferences;
- that judgement about potentially complex issues may be impaired;
- that understanding of new ideas and information may be difficult;
- that they are unlikely to have insight into their own situations and therefore require protection.

These kind of assumptions appear to underpin much recent practice with regard to people with dementia. And it is, perhaps, because of the difficulty of understanding people in this user group that much of the thinking and literature has typically focused on the needs of carers and the 'burdens' of caring (Mace and Rabins 1985; Holden, Martin and White 1984; Marshall 1992). It is disconcerting that the literature on involving users with dementia is so sparse. In 1993 the National Health Service Training Directorate published 'Users and Carers: A Directory of Resources'. Within this document there was no mention of any resource for the need for participation by people with dementia.

Departmental guidance from the Department of Health also appears to lack clarity about how best to approach the needs of this group of people. On the one hand the Care Programme Approach is considered the appropriate one for people referred to specialist psychiatric services, which, of course, includes people with dementia. This approach, focusing on assessment and robust care plans for discharge and after care, includes 'monitoring' and 'keeping in contact' (LASSL (90) 11; HC/90/23). It gives the health authority lead responsibility and user involvement is limited to 'the need to involve patients and carers in discussions about care programmes'. Research indicates that in practice consultation often takes place at ward rounds for people who may temporarily be in-patients, and many people find this intimidating (North, Richie and Ward 1993). One hospital manager is quoted as saying 'case programme approach is a way of identifying those people who are most ill, most likely to upset the Member of Parliament or the neighbours and to try and identify these needs...' furthermore, who gets admitted to hospital is a somewhat random process, depending on social and health factors, as well as the availability of bed space.

Assessment of older people with dementia can occur either in a community or a hospital setting. As yet there is no research to evaluate the consequences and outcomes of assessments occurring in these different environments. The matter of where an older person is assessed still appears to be largely a matter of chance. The alternative approach of care management where social service departments have the lead role emphasizes to a greater degree needs-led assessment, which involves user participation and subsequent choice in care planning. Where it is deemed to be not feasible to involve users in this process, for whatever reason, the services of an advocate are officially encouraged. However, none of these approaches appears to recognize the difficulties of reaching a genuine understanding of the needs and preferences of people with dementia.

With regard to advocacy – now officially recognized in numerous reports issued by the Department of Health – unless an advocate has known somebody and has great empathy with them over a long period, it is unlikely they will understand a user's preferences especially if they are experiencing moderate/severe dementia unless there is, or has recently been, genuine communication between them. Therefore, advocacy defined as speaking *on behalf of* another person may constitute a very partial solution if these prerequisites have not been satisfied. Furthermore, there are practical difficulties in ensuring a suitable supply of advocates for people with dementia. Such issues are developed further in recent publications (Ivers 1994; Dunning 1995)

The recent Law Commission Report and draft legislation on mental incapacity recommends a new 'continuing power of Attorney' to replace the existing somewhat unsatisfactory situation of 'powers' and 'enduring powers' of Attorney (Law Commission 1995). This change would allow for a named representative in matters pertaining not only to finance but also to welfare issues. Similar considerations to those outlined above would also seem to apply in connection with this: that the done would need to know the donor very well in order to adequately convey and represent their views. Substitute decision making may not be easy to secure and operationalize for this group of elders.

If user choice cannot be articulated – or more likely cannot be understood by the receiver of the communication – can there be consent to any plan of action or any basis for a contract? Marsh and Fisher (1992) suggest that 'passive consent', i.e. acceptance as opposed to challenge or disagreement, is as far as one can go in adhering to basic principles of partnership – as opposed to imposition of externally mandated work – when working with people with dementia. This approach implies minimal negotiation or two-way communication and cannot be considered as essentially needs-based or involving choices. Two-way communication, I would suggest, is the key component for understanding another person and formulating a person-centred, need-based approach.

Professional Dilemmas

How does this leave front-line professionals in their attempts to provide needs-based assessment? For many practitioners, they will probably experience something of a quandary. Will they be acting *ultra vires* in making plans *on behalf of* people with dementia? Should they be thinking of guardianship as a more appropriate route? However, guardianship only confers very specific powers and not those that are particularly related to individual preferences. Is there a ready supply of advocates both willing and able to develop long-term relationships, communicate with and understand the individual and yet be totally independent of all family considerations? This would seem to be an unlikely scenario.

To reiterate the key issues in this paper: is it feasible for people with dementia themselves to participate in assessment and care planning or, alternatively, to participate actively in influencing their care and living arrangements and activities?

Awareness and Capacity To Communicate

To begin to attempt to answer this question one needs to be clear about the awareness and comprehension of the individual person with regard to themselves and their circumstances and their capacity to communicate (in whatever form) their views. This is, of course, likely to vary on a wide range of dimensions but particularly according to the stage of the illness that is affecting the person. Nonetheless, the admittedly sparse evidence that we have at present points to an ability to communicate both verbally and non-verbally and to a continued awareness and sensitivity to personal issues and hence a continuing sense of self and personhood – even in the later stages of dementia (Kitwood 1993; Shortt 1990; National Consumer Council 1987). The growing evidence suggests that we cannot say our actions will have no effect on people with dementia even at a late stage of the illness or that the choices that are made concerning them will be unimportant to the person who is affected by them. Therefore, sensitivity to the person would appear to be essential at all stages of care planning processes and the users' views and preferences, whether or not they can be articulated clearly, would seem to be very important.

Communication and People with Dementia

The key issue it would appear then is not whether these users' views are important but how indeed we might equip ourselves better to understand and obtain them. Dementia may be typified by low levels of concentration, aphasia and poor short-term memory but these difficulties do not in themselves preclude communication. They do, however, require a very skilled and sensitive listener and communicator who can become accustomed to an individual's patterns of speech and who then develops appropriate communication techniques for that particular individual (Stokes and Goudie 1992). Communication, of course, occurs at verbal and non-verbal levels and understanding is enhanced by familiarity between two people. Empathy, which has been defined as 'person's ability to communicate understanding; to understand what the other person is thinking and feeling, their perception of the situation and what they want' (Smale and Tuson 1993) can only be developed over a lengthy period of time if verbal communication is impaired. The National Consumer Council (NCC) study on users' views involved interviewing people with moderate/severe dementia. This demonstrated that even at a fairly late stage people with dementia could indeed communicate if workers listened actively, used an ethnographic and reflexive method of communication and if they assumed that the user was the expert rather than themselves (NCC 1987). However, at the present time we are at a very early stage in developing the skill of understanding and communicating with people with later-stage dementia who are experiencing communication difficulties.

The Importance of Early Intervention

Given the present state of social work/care manager knowledge and skill concerning successful communication and understanding of people with moderate/severe dementia, this would seem to point critically to the importance of early intervention. An early assessment, which would include an extensive biography or life history, would facilitate understanding the 'whole person'. Indeed, knowledge of the person and their biography may prove a prerequisite for subsequent communication and understanding as the disease progresses. The ability to empathize, understand and communicate may rely on recognizing not only speech patterns but also, somewhat more fundamentally, the personality and attitudes of the person. All of this would seem to have implications not only for social workers/care managers but also for advocates if they are genuinely committed to speaking 'on behalf of the person' rather than using their own assumptions, however well meaning. Equally, such considerations appear to be of importance when considering the use of substitute judgement in decision making for elders who lack capacity. It can also be argued that 'substitute judgements', that is to say judgements which are based on personal knowledge of a person acquired over a period of time, are likely to be more appropriate to the user than mere assumption of what they want. However, if genuine empathy occurs between worker and user at an early stage of the illness it may be more likely that this understanding will continue over time and genuine communication continue more effectively over the course of the illness. In these types of instances, it may be possible to retain the ability to ascertain the actual views of the individual rather than the implied or assumed view obtained via a substitute judgement.

It could be argued that carers may have this kind of knowledge and therefore could advocate on behalf of the user (or potential user). This may be the case in some circumstances but it would be naïve to be unaware of actual or potential conflicts of interests concerning a users' views or preferences. Carers may perceive themselves to be well placed to exercise substitute judgements on behalf of the person they care for but in any event this must surely be a 'second best' approach as compared with the person's reaction or one based on direct communication that is understood. It is only through direct communication that the person and their experience can be genuinely understood and validated. The Law Commission's consultation paper on mentally incapacitated adults recognized this potential tension in their view that carers should not assume an automatic right to take decisions on behalf of the person being cared for merely on the basis of the caring relationship (Law Commission 1993).

The policy implications of our presently very partial understanding of people with dementia indicate that a partnership approach should ideally be built on a relationship that starts at an early stage of the disease process. Given current levels of staff turnover, there would also seem to be a case for precise documentation and sharing of information regarding the person and their lifestyle and preferences. As with other user groups there needs to be understanding of the whole person: the person's biography, views and preferences as well as an understanding of developing speech patterns. At an early stage a key worker or care manager could begin to build this profile of the whole person which could form the basis of future work both between themselves and the user and/or with other professionals. This kind of record could be called up at a later stage when communication may become more difficult. In this case quality work should be seen as early intervention – not necessarily as in other instances as preventative work but to ensure future quality contact and genuine understanding and communication. Although recognizing there may be confidentiality issues on sharing information, there would seem to be clear practical advantages to closer co-ordination between professionals and especially with a professional or key worker who has achieved a genuinely empathic relationship.

Conclusion

Can user involvement and choice apply to people with dementia? This chapter suggests a qualified 'yes' if assessment is ongoing, if communication established early in the disease process, if continuity of information and relationships are valued and if self determination is seen as not only possible but appropriate for people with dementia. This is not to suggest that all people will be able to make difficult judgements about a range of issues including decisions regarding the types of services to be received when they find complex information difficult to manage. This kind of decision does, perhaps, need to be made earlier and, perhaps, endorsed through procedures such as living wills or advance directives of the sort suggested in the Law Commission report (Law Commission 1995). It does suggest, however, that, given adequate communication skills, professionals who have established empathy with users should be able to understand the concerns, views and lifestyle preferences of those with dementia until a late stage of the illness. In achieving this they will be offering a needs-based service that involves the user. A service where the user can positively influence their care and living arrangements.

In view of the likelihood that the first of point of contact for people with dementia is the GP, and the now well defined responsibility of the GP is to offer assessments to the over 75 age group of patients, it is suggested that it ought to be possible to detect dementia at an earlier stage than presently seems to be the case. The development of specialist community based dementia teams may also assist in this regard. The early detection and identification of dementia could be utilized by the wider primary care team to initiate the biographical assessment process and also to ensure a multi-disciplinary approach to the needs of the individual with a key worker or care manager identified.

At this early stage the individual user could be requested to give permission for this profiling work to be undertaken. If necessary, the information obtained could then be handed on to advocates, professionals and others involved as the disease progresses. Indeed, contained within this information would most likely be the views and preferences on care, living and lifestyle arrangements which are clearly essential requirements for appropriate user-led care planning.

References

Croft, S. and Beresford, P. (1990) *From Paternalism to Participation: Involving People in Social Services.* London: Open Services Project.

DOH (1990) *Community Care in the Next Decade and Beyond.* London: HMSO.

DOH (1990) *The Care Programme Approach for People Referred to Specialist Psychiatric Services.* London: HMSO. (HC, 90/23; LASSL (90)).

Dunning, A. (1995) *Citizen Advocacy with Older People: A Code of Good Practice.* London: Centre for Policy on Ageing.

Holden, U., Martin, C. and White, M. (1984) *Twenty Four Hour Approach to the Problems of Confusion in Elderly People*. Winslow, Bucks: Winslow Press.

Ivers, V. (1994) *Citizen Advocacy in Action: Working with Older People*. Stoke on Trent: Beth Johnson Foundation.

Jorm, A.F. (1987) *Understanding Senile Dementia*. London: Croom Helm.

Kitwood, T. and Bredin, P. (1992) 'Towards a theory of dementia care: personhood and wellbeing.' *Ageing and Society 12, 3*, 269–287.

Law Commission (1993) *Mentally Incapacitated Adults and Decision Making: A New Jurisdiction*, Consultation Paper no. 128. London: HMSO.

Local Authority Social Services Letter 1990/11. Health Circular 1990/23.

Law Commission (1995) *Mental Incapacity*. London: HMSO.

Mace, N.L. and Rabins, P. (1985) *The 36 Hour Day*. London: Age Concern/Edward Arnold.

Marsh, P. and Fisher, M. (1992) *Good Intentions: Developing Partnership in Social Services*. York: Rowntree.

Marshall, M. (1990) *Working with Dementia*. Birmingham: Venture Press.

National Consumer Council (1987) *Consulting Consumers in the NHS*. London: NCC

North, C., Ritchie, J. and Ward, K. (1993) *Factors Influencing the Implementation of the Care Programme Approach*. London: HMSO.

NHS Training Directorate (1993) *Involving Users and Carers: A Directory of Resources*. London: HMSO.

Oliver, M. (1990) *The Politics of Disablement*. Basingstoke: Macmillan.

Shortt, S. (1990) *Facts, Myth and Power: The Social Construction of Senile Dementia*. London: Social Care Association.

Smale, G. and Tuson, G. (1993) *Empowerment, Assessment, Care Management and the Skilled Worker*. London: NISW House.

Stokes, G. and Goudie, F. (1990) *Working with Dementia*. Winslow, Bucks: Winslow Press.

CHAPTER 7

Research, Theory and Practice
Misunderstanding Verbal Language During Community Care Assessments

David Barrett

Summary

It has been observed during a recent research programme with older people (Barrett 1992) that verbal language has been used in several different ways (Language, for the purposes of this discussion, has been interpreted within a sociocultural context (Halliday 1978, p.2).

Probably the work of Mead (1934), is the most useful as a starting point in attempting to illuminate this area in seeking greater understanding of how language is used symbolically by older people. What is expressed explicitly may not be the same as what is implied. Therefore, different levels of meaning exist (Gumperz and Cook-Gumperz 1988, p.130).

This chapter argues that some parts of verbal language are used as a defence and a coping mechanism in a way that obscures the everyday realities of the low level of existence in which these older people live. It forms the basis of a rationalization, a good reason but not the real reason of self-description and can repress or ignore the unpleasantness of a day to day existence.

This notion of using language as a coping and/or a defence mechanism, when transferred to the arena of community care assessments, takes a very worrying turn because what is being said may not be what is meant. Coded messages (See Coupland 1991; Barrett 1993 and 1993a for examples), may be given throughout an assessment interview. It is argued here that 'coded messages' could be a trigger in their own right for workers to look beyond presenting problems during assessments. Additionally, senior managers in health and welfare organizations need to understand what complex tasks they are asking their 'front line' workers to undertake and they should organize their workers' work schedules accordingly.

Introduction

How does an examination of verbal language and its every day usage lead to a more enlightened view of what complex tasks community care assessments are? In this chapter a research programme is examined and some of the subsequent linguistic issues and arguments are explored before making the connection with older people and their community care assessors. The latter is then explored in the context of some of the current processes and principles that underpin the present welfare state. When looked at from this perspective assessments are remarkably complex interactions. Are they recognized as such?

Research: The Research Programme

One major consequence of research in the area of the use of language is that the different interpretations placed upon meanings can give cause for concern. For example, how those workers carrying out community care assessments perceive and interpret what is said to them by the older people they are assessing.

First, however, it is necessary to provide a few background details about the research programme. It was essentially a qualitative-oriented PhD research programme that was exploring some of the issues concerning poorer older people and community care. The data was collected between 1988 and 1990 and was primarily transcripts of in-depth interviews which adhered to a schedule that the author developed with some older people. Forty respondents were involved in the programme and were chosen on a 'snowballing' basis (20 in a rural setting in and around Redbourn in Hertfordshire and 20 in an inner-city setting in Luton, Bedfordshire). One of the variables that became more significant as the programme progressed was the economic position of the older people. Each of the 40 respondents was classified on an economic basis, either they were economically fragile (those who were totally reliant on the state for their income) or they were not economically fragile (those with other income in addition to the state income, e.g. occupational pensions, investments).

One of the manifestations of this distinction between the economic groups was that there appeared to be some noticeable differences in the meanings attached to some key words in the transcripts.[1] For the purposes of this paper and in order to explore the language issue in some detail the term 'managing' is selected for closer scrutiny, both because it appears to portray this most accurately and also because it has wide implications in terms of its influence. Some of the contexts in which the term 'managing' was used are outlined below. These are taken from the transcripts of the interviews with the two respective groups of respondents as outlined above. A different emphasis is, however, apparent.

For the non-economically fragile older people 'managing' seems to mean: acting within a longer term view, within the spirit of a positive outlook to future life chances. Examples from the research (respondents 13, 35 and 36), say respectively: 'Oh yes, I do manage on my money'; 'I couldn't manage if there wasn't a bit in the bank'; 'You've got to manage'. For the economically fragile 'managing' seems to mean acting within a shorter term view, in the context of existing and just "getting-by", and within the spirit of a negative outlook to future life chances. Such examples (Respondents 17, 18 and 30), say respectively: 'We manage week by week but there's nothing to spare'; 'We're managing at the moment'; 'We get by, we manage.'[1]

What might these differences in the use of language on the grounds of economic circumstances mean? Could it affect an older person's life? Could it be symbolic of other features in the lives of these older people? These are some of the questions that are to be addressed and explored within this chapter.

Theory: Linguistics, Semiotic Analysis and Older People

Probably the work of Mead (1934), is the most useful as a starting point in attempting to illuminate this area in seeking greater understanding of how this part of language is used by the older people in the sample. Mead stressed the importance and centrality of language and the use of symbols in social life. He gave more attention to small-scale processes than wider society and his model of work came to be known as symbolic interactionism.

Mead argued that reflexivity was fundamental to the development of self as a social phenomenon. Social life depends on our ability not only to imagine ourselves in other social roles but, also, when taking one role or the other, it depends on our capacity for an internal conversation with ourselves. Mead conceived society as an exchange of gestures which involves the use of symbols. Symbolic interactionism thus becomes a self-society relationship as a process of symbolic communications between social actors (Rock 1979).

This perspective has important contributions to make in the analysis of older people in contemporary society. For example, in the conclusion to the previously mentioned research (Barrett 1992), questions were raised around the current stigmatization, role defining and socialization processes that older people are involved in and how this might be linked to a possible predictable 'career path' for some older people based on their economic position. The role of language may be symptomatic or indicative of wider social processes and influences currently at work.

It can be argued that the symbols expressed in speech are the most important way in which human meanings are formed and expressed, for language is perhaps the most distinctive of all human cultural attributes. But, without wanting to get too involved in the idiosyncrasies of the social semiotics of language, the way in which language is constructed is important

---

1   Further details about coding methodology can be obtained from the author at: Department of Professional Social Studies, University of Luton, Park Square, Luton, Beds, LU1 3JU.

here. What is expressed explicitly may not be the same as what is implied. Therefore different levels of meaning exist.

Gumperz and Cook-Gumperz (1988, p.130), usefully set the tone for such a discussion: 'Our basic premise is that social processes are symbolic processes but that symbols have meaning only in relation to the forces which control the utilization and allocation of environmental resources. We customarily take gender, ethnicity and class as given parameters and boundaries within which we create our own social identities. The study of language as interactional discourse demonstrates that these parameters are not constants that can be taken for granted but are communicatively produced. Therefore, to understand such issues of identity and how they are affected by social, political and ethnic divisions we need to gain insights into the communicative processes by which they arise.'

Society consists of participants but, perhaps, more important than the individual participants, is the relationships they have, for these relations define social roles. Halliday (1978, p.14), says: 'Being a member of society means occupying a social role; and it is again by means of language that a 'person' becomes potentially the occupant of a social role'. He goes on to discuss the general functions of language, the first is most relevant to this chapter and is thus worth quoting in full:

> Language has to interpret the whole of our experience, reducing the indefinitely varied phenomena of the world around us, and also of the world inside us, the processes of our own consciousness, to a manageable number of classes of phenomena: types of processes, events and actions, classes of objects, people and institutions, and the like. (Halliday 1978, p.21)

Bernstein (1971) has taken this view a stage further. He argued that in order to understand the social system it is important to understand the crucial role language plays in this. He approached this by considering the role language plays in the socialization process and the more general social theory of cultural transmission and the maintenance of the social system. Although Bernstein started from a social structure perspective, sometimes his ideas are presented as conflicting with the linguistic structure as the starting point to analysis (Halliday 1978, p.2).

Saussure (1974), in an essentially ahistorical approach, argued that the meaning of words derives from the structures of language and not necessarily from the objects to which the words refer. Meaning is created by the differences between related concepts which the rules of language recognize. However, a cautionary observation is worth remembering about Saussure's approach: 'Here, all is still and patterned. To take history out of any study is to remove the need for causal explanations; what is left can be seen as structured, and only structures have importance' (Levitt 1992, p.38).

Meanings are thus created internally within language and not strictly by the objects in the world to which we refer. This may account for the variations in meaning over time and regions. There seems to be some flexibility then in how widely language may be interpreted. Gumperz and Cook-Gumperz argue that the changing nature of communities affects the way people relate to each other: 'The old forms of plural society in which families lived in island-like communities, surrounded and supported by others of similar ethnic or class background, are no longer typical. In our daily lives we have become increasingly dependent on public services and on co-operation with others who may not share our culture' (Gumperz and Cook-Gumperz 1988, p.131)

What of the analysis of language in relation to older people? The most widely known and recent works are by Coupland, Coupland and Giles (1991) who follow the sociolinguistic tradition. Apart from noting the lack of attention that language analysis in the context of older people has received, one of the most interesting aspects of their work is the discourse-centred analyses of interaction which, they claim, is a means of displaying social construction processes in action (1991a pp.55–6).

At these different levels of understanding the term 'managing' can clearly have different levels of meaning and be relatively fluid. An analysis in this context would suggest that it is the differences that create the meaning and not simply the meanings as they appear at face value. For example, in the two views of 'managing' above, from the different economic starting points, there appears two very clear differences in the language itself. First, between 'to bring about successfully' and 'attempt to bring about successfully', and second, between the negative and the positive aspects associated within the meaning. The spirit of the application of both is perhaps the final dimension to the differences. What matters then is not the literal meaning but the differences. Here the older people who are economically fragile use the term 'managing' differently from the so-called 'normal' understanding of the term. This approach has its origins in the structuralist approach to sociology and anthropology (Levi-Strauss 1958).

It seems then that this different use of the term 'managing' when seen from the perspective of the economically fragile group can be viewed in two ways. First, the term 'managing' does mean only existing on a day to day basis with no prospect of a positive future. Second, the underlying meaning could be the exact opposite of the more normal understanding of the term manage (i.e. 'to control: to contrive successfully: to manipulate: to bring about' [Chambers Dictionary]). These meanings seem a long way from the everyday experiences of poor older people.

Practice: Verbal Language and Community Care Assessments

It seems that different uses of every day terms and parts of language may be used in different ways. For example, poorer older people may be overly deferential to the visiting professional and may therefore use language, either consciously or unconsciously, as a defence and a coping mechanism in a way that obscures the everyday realities of the low level of existence in which they live. It forms the basis of a rationalization, a good reason, but not the real reason, of self-description. To face the reality would probably result in these people acknowledging that they are not managing or coping, it is a way of repressing or ignoring the unpleasantness of a day to day existence.

This notion of using language as a coping and/or a defence mechanism, when transferred to the arena of community care assessments, takes a very worrying turn because what is being said may not be what is meant. For example, in addition to some older people still being overly deferential to the helping professionals they may talk and respond to them in coded messages throughout an assessment interview. The idea of asking 'the welfare' for help also remains an anathema to some too. Some key phrases (see Barrett 1993 and 1993a for examples) could be triggers in their own right for assessment workers to look beyond presenting problems, albeit in their own pressurized work environments, and consider other forms of evidence that may indicate underlying problems, especially for those in the economically fragile group – those totally reliant on the state for their income (Barrett 1993a).

Most people know that older people should not have to 'manage' in a welfare state but the nature of the present welfare state is important here. Currently it seems to be underpinned by a wobbly industrial capitalism, requiring the constant expansion of production and a perpetual increasing of wealth. The total cost of the former, and not only in financial terms, and the distribution of the latter are the subject of considerable debate. This is essentially a political debate. As Giddens (1989, p.643) stated: '...activities of political leaders and government officials constantly affect the lives of the mass of the population. Both externally and internally, political decision-making promotes and directs social change far more than in previous times'. This includes economic growth and the style in which it is undertaken. The state then has a high level of influence on both 'the system' and the individuals within it.

This type of large and societal issue seems far removed from that of the meaning of language, a relatively small cog in the large wheel of life. There are many variable concepts which make up the socio-semiotic theory of language, varying from the text itself to the situation and social structure does have an important role to play within this context.

Gumperz and Cook-Gumperz argue that with the continuing polarization of society, misunderstandings and misrepresentations happen. They suggest: 'when this situation persists over time, what starts as isolated situation-bound communication differences at the individual level may harden into ideological distinctions that then become value laden, so that every time problems of understanding arise they serve to create further differences in the symbolization of identity' (Gumperz and Cook-Gumperz 1988, p.131).

Conclusion: Considerations for the Future

More important, however, I hope this discussion contributes to a greater understanding of what a complex task and process community care assessments are. Adequate time must be allowed for proper and thorough assessments, especially of complex situations. Therefore, senior managers need to allow sufficient time for such complex work when allocating time schedules for their staff who undertake assessments. Additionally, staff need to allow sufficient time for assessments, including time to prepare and to attend to linguistic issues within the assessment process.

As an eminent linguistics scholar reminds us when discussing older people and language 'damaging stereotypes still lurk in the gerontological undergrowth' (Levitt 1992, p.42). Speedy assessments in 'child protection work' are no longer viewed as acceptable. Nor should they be in work with older people, whether this surrounds issues of vulnerability or protection or not. They are a manifestation of ageist practice and should be avoided.

People in positions of power in both health and welfare service provision should, one hopes, be considering their positions and professional decision making carefully. Front-line workers who undertake assessments need support with their task. Those involved, particularly in senior management positions, must be able to interpret the language and hear the message!

References

Barrett, D. (1992) *Community Care: The Impact of Current Welfare Policies and Ideologies on Older People in Herts/Beds*. PhD thesis: Middlesex University.

Barrett, D. (1993) 'But you told me you were managing! The use of language as a defence mechanism.' *Journal of Educational Gerontology* April, 1993.

Barrett, D. (1993a) *Older People, Poverty and Community Care Under the Tories*. Aldershot: Avebury.

Bernstein, B. (1971) *Class, Codes and Control: Theoretical Studies Towards a Sociology of Language*. London: Routledge and Kegan Paul.

Coupland, N.J. and Giles, H. (eds) (1991) 'Sociolinguistic Issues in Ageing.' *Ageing and Society*, (special issue), 11, 2.

Coupland, N.J. and Giles, H. (1991a) *Language, Society and the Elderly: Discourse Identity and Ageing*. Oxford: Blackwell.

Giddens, A. (1989) *Sociology*. London: Polity Press.

Gumperz, J. and Cook-Gumperz, J. (1988) 'Language and the communication of social identity.' In N. Mercer (ed) *Language and Literacy I*. Buckingham: Open University Press.

Halliday, M. (1978) *Language as Social Semiotic*. London: Edward Arnold.

Levi-Strauss, C. (1958) *Structural Anthropology*. London: Allen Lane.

Levitt, J. (1992) 'Linguistics and older people.' *Journal of Educational Gerontology 7, 1*, 36–43.

Mead, G. (1934) *Mind, Self and Society*. Chicago: Chicago University Press.
Rock, P. (1979) *The Making of Symbolic Interactionism*. Basingstoke: Macmillan.
Saussure, F. (1974) *Course in General Linguistics*. London: Fontana.

CHAPTER 8

The Effects of Care Management on Efficiency in Long-Term Care
A New Evaluation Model Applied to British and American Data

*Bleddyn Davies, Barry Baines
and John Chesterman*

This chapter has three aims. The first is to sharpen theoretical argument and empirical research on the costs and benefits of alternative combinations of case management and other care inputs. Its results illustrate the importance of making the logics more precise. The second it is to re-evaluate the impact of the leading American case management experiment in the light of the argument. The results show that this sharper theoretical perspective puts the outcomes of the experiment in a new light. The third is to use the framework applied to new evidence to draw conclusions for the implementation of budget-devolved care management in the United Kingdom.

Context

Particularly in the UK, one stream of British case management argument has been turning from evaluating the potential of the care management approach to developing evidence and argument to help the matching arrangements for the performance of core case management tasks to the needs-related circumstances of users and the characteristics of area systems (Challis 1993; Davies 1992; Davies, Bebbington, Charnley and colleagues 1990). That will become increasingly important as local authorities turn their attention to developing their case management systems.

Case management arrangements and performance differs greatly. Therefore, it will be important for such evaluations to discern the effects of the case management arrangements treated separately and in combination. However, in the past, outcome evaluations have not assessed the impact of variations in case management 'arrangements and parameters'[1] themselves,

---

1   Case management 'arrangements' are broad structural characteristics set mainly in advance and changeable only periodically. Case management parameters are variables, often changeable in the short run. See Davies, Bebbington, Charnley and colleagues (1990) and Davies (1992).

but the impact of programmes which embody 'case management' often of an ill-defined form, programmes which also have other (equally ill-defined) features.[2] Among the parameters whose effects are most important to explore is the quantity of case management input itself. That parameter is the main focus of this chapter.

To separate out the contribution of case management, we must return to basic theory. Exactly how does case management with the authority and influence to secure more subtle, equitable and efficient responses to clients needs and wishes work?

Theory

The starting point is that 'marginal productivities' of case management and other inputs vary. Therefore, reflecting the first order conditions for optimization, managers must seek to equalize the ratios of inputs of case management and other inputs to their relative prices if they are to make the best use of resources (Henderson and Quandt 1980, p.76). That meta-theory is well established; the essential background to this, as to other issues, surrounds choosing the best combination of inputs.

The most general postulate of case management argument is that there are ranges of case management inputs and inputs of the other resources consumed by community-based care, over which an increase in the inputs of case management can decrease the costs of beneficial outcomes enough to make increasing inputs of home care worth while. It follows that under some circumstances, the inputs of case management reduces the costs of outcomes obtained from other community-based services.

A more complicated form of the argument is perhaps more valid:

1. Case management inputs can contribute to the production of outcomes both directly[3] and indirectly, and the indirect contribution is made by improving efficiency of all five kinds in the use of other resources.

2. The marginal productivity curves for case management inputs and for other home care services depend on one another.

2   Examples are the summaries of the views of the evaluation consultants in the Australian national report on the evaluation of Community Options projects, the examples scattered through the process report of the channelling experiments, the large number of articles by those who describe features of case management practice (Applebaum and Austin, 1989; Challis and Davies, 1986, Chapters 3–6; Davies and Challis, 1986, Chapters 6–8). But these are low level generalizations. See the detailed discussion of the nature of the evaluations of case management projects around the world in Davies (1992) and the summary comments on the American evaluations in Davies (1992).

3   This is illustrated by the way in which users of the CMP appreciated the style of their treatment by advocates (misleadingly named case managers) with little influence on resources, though the users had strong reservations about the degree to which the 'case managers' actually influenced the supply of resources, as Doria Pilling (1988, pp.3, 4) showed. (The results of this and other projects in which case managers have weak authority over resources is discussed in Davies, Bebbington and Charnley; 1990, p.335–6.)

Figure 8.1 shows the postulated shapes of the productivity curves for case management inputs (given the level of other inputs) and other community service inputs (given the level of case management inputs).[4] HOMEDUR is taken as the dependent variable because of the importance of shifting the balance of care mode in the White Paper on community care.

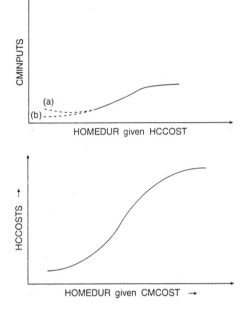

Care management inputs (CMINPUTS), other costs of community-based social and community health care (HCCOSTS), and average duration of stay in the community (HOMEDUR).

Figure 8.1   Care management inputs, other costs of community-based social and community health services and average duration of stay in the community: postulated relationships

4   Figure 8.1 is the core of the formal model described in pp. 366–377 of Davies, Bebbington, Charnley and colleagues (1990) and Appendix 2 of Davies (1992). The south-east quadrant of the diagram in that appendix hypothesises the implications of two levels of case management inputs (traced through from case management loads given case mix to the costs of case management, CMCOST) for the effects of different levels of other home care costs for duration of stay at home. (The diagram is a summary of the logic connecting case management arrangements and home care costs to residential utilization, and so back to the level of home care costs beyond which equivalent outcomes are more cost-effectively obtained. To express the logic diagrammatically, it has been necessary to reverse directions on some axes including the axes in the south-east quadrant.)

The southeast quadrant therefore has two curves corresponding to the second part of Figure 8.1. It asserts that comparing low CMCOST (for instance, as low as in standard British home care) with higher CMCOST (say at the level of the PSSRU experiments), (i) the average HCCOST of a level of HOMEDUR will be higher, and (ii) that the cost of an increase of one unit of HOMEDUR will also be higher. That is, both the average and marginal costs of HOMEDUR will be greater with very low than with moderately high CMCOST.

The first part of Figure 8.1 suggests a likely shape for the relationship between the level of inputs of case management and the highest common factor of nearly all case management evaluations, the duration of stay at home (HOMEDUR) rather than in some form of residential care. At very low levels of input of case management, additions might increase the probability of admission to institutions for long-term care for some user groups. The reason is that at extremely low levels, it is often the case that no one manages the careful work needed in some contexts to help people to make an appropriate choice to enter a home, and to help in subsequent processes. But, in general, the greater the case management input, the more the impact of the home care services on duration of stay at home. It is not necessary to describe the processes in entrepreneurial and user-focused case management because they have been repeatedly described for work in this country, and are described for other countries also (Goodman 1981; Kanter 1989; Moxley 1989; Australian Department of Health, Housing and Community Services 1992; Howe, Ozanne and Selby-Smith 1992; Applebaum and Austin 1990). However, case management can yield diminishing returns.

The position and slope of the curve depends partly on the level of other service inputs postulated. Also, as we have argued above, the way case management is undertaken depends crucially on broader features of the programme of which it is dependent, and the broader context of that programme.

The second part of Figure 8.1 postulates a similar general shape for the effects of other inputs of community services, (OTHHCCOSTS). Again, increases by small amounts do not have large effects on the population most at risk at low levels of inputs. There is a larger effect at higher ranges, but these effects tail off.[5]

Approaches to Testing and Estimation

There are at least two approaches to be taken into account. One consists of direct observations of differences between programmes in the impacts of variations in case management inputs on the marginal productivities or costs. The (inferior) kind of evidence consists of the impact of variations within programmes on marginal productivities or costs. The second type is inferior because in effect it depends on errors of judgement and other causes of suboptimization by the case managers.

---

5   The relative positions and slopes of the two curves in Figure 8.1 are too dependent on the
     case mix postulated for the geometry of the parts of the diagram to be finely drawn.
     However, it has been attempted to draw the diagram in such a way that with
     medium-high CMCOST and HCCOSTS, the relative spending on case management and
     other community-based services broadly correspond to the experience in the Sheppey
     community care programme.

The Empirical Analysis

Logic Outlined

The basic logic of the first approach is that we use evidence for a fully-evaluated model applied in a controlled and, so as far as is possible in an imperfect world, in a standardized way, in enough sites to allow the site itself to be a unit in a statistical analysis. Then, having taken further steps to control for variations between the sites, we test for a correlation between caseload size and the outcome in question.

First, the data set. It is from the evaluation of the American Long-Term Care Channelling Project.[6] The channelling project was implemented in ten sites with determined efforts to achieve standardization and with an extremely rich outcomes evaluation undertaken with high professional competence. It was the biggest and best-evaluated American case management experiment. Attempts were made to establish case management of a good standard in it.

There was another good reason for taking the channelling data set. The evaluators reported that the number of cases per case manager was at levels at which there would be clear benefits from increased case manager input. For instance, Carcagno *et al.* (1986, p.267) wrote:

> Case managers reported being frustrated at being unable to monitor their full caseload; and some discussed instances in which clients experienced major changes (such as being hospitalized for a long period, or a provider changing services) without the case manager being aware of them. In general, case managers felt that the amount of time they had for ongoing case management was not adequate given the typical channelling client. This concern was shared by a number of providers...

Second, controlling for site variations. The method allows for the most important source of variations in apparent outcomes: variations in the need-related circumstances of users. It does so by fitting a 'production function' for the experiment. The production function estimates the effects of service inputs on outcomes, controlling for the effects of need-related circumstances. It describes how which outcomes are, on average, produced from given inputs. The production function is then used to predict outcomes for each site. The difference between what the experiment-wide production function estimated and what was observed for each site then measures the degree to which the site was more or less successful than average.

Third, estimating the effects of variations in caseload size on site outcomes. The correlation between differences between actual and predicted outcomes is studied. These differences we call the residuals. The final stage

---

6   The PSSRU community care projects most like the original Kent Community Care Project are now far enough advanced for us to start treating them as a multi-site experiment.

is, therefore, the prediction of the residuals from the site caseloads, using regression analysis.

So much for the general logic. I shall now elaborate each step in the analysis undertaken.

Controlling Site Variations

A production function has been estimated to control for site variations. The argument embodied in Figure 8.1 focuses on HOMEDUR as the criterion of success. However, HOMEDUR is not directly estimable from the channelling data. An 'excess' of actual admissions over predicted admissions would be strongly negatively correlated with it. So, the dependent variable of the production function is the probability of admission to nursing homes.

The first serious American attempt at the estimation of a production function for care was based on the channelling set by Vernon Greene (1992; 1993). Ingeniously, he based the analysis on movements during each month of the three-year evaluation, and used the probabilities of moves each month as his outcome indicator. Although our model is built on Greene's modelling, our models differed from his because they are based only on the experimental groups.

Greene's production function is compared with ours in Table 8.1. The results were higher estimates of the coefficients reflecting the marginal productivities of the main home care services than yielded by Greene, implying that the additive forms used by Greene (and all the other modelling analyses and reanalyses of the channelling data known to the author) may underestimate impacts because – as is implicit in case management theory outlined above, and the argument of Davies *et al.* (1990, pp.291–3) – case management works by affecting the influence of each unit of home care resource by targeting it better and by other means.

The production function was applied to all cases in all sites. The difference between the actual observations and those predicted from the production function were estimated.

In practice, the way in which variations in caseload would affect probabilities of admission to institutions for long-term care would be by making it more or less feasible for the case managers to concentrate attention on the minority facing a crisis likely to result in preventable admission during that month. Carcagno *et al.* were aware of this fundamental feature of the case management of clients with volatile needs: '...some proportion of the caseload was always experiencing a crisis (such as illness of the caregiver, client health problems, provider problems) which required substantial case manager involvement. Indeed, case managers indicated that a major component of ongoing case management actually involved crisis management or problem resolution' (Carcagno 1986, p.267). So one should not be looking for the effect of caseload size on the average residual over all cases in the site. The case managers would focus their attention on the minority with a

Table 8.1 Logit Prediction of Probabilities of Transition from the Community to Nursing Home

Logit coefficients

Predictor	Greene estimate	Baines/Davies estimate
Inputs		
Community nursing	-.091	-.305^{xxx}
Community nursing of persons in wheelchair	-.306^{x}	-.867^{xxx}
Home health service of cognitively impaired person	-.028^{xx}	
Personal care service x ADL score interaction	-.007^{xx}	-.030^{xxx}
Housekeeper service x ADL score interaction	-.033^{x}	-.060^{xxx}
Housekeeper service	-.021	-.037^{xx}
User Circumstances		
Afro-American	-.709^{xxx}	-.338^{xxx}
Hispanic-American	-.838^{xxx}	-.616^{xx}
Female	-0.82	
Age	-.009	.020^{xxx}
Houseowner	-.316^{xxx}	-1.554^{xxx}
Lives alone	.462^{xxx}	.326^{xxx}
Extremely or very severe ADL problems	.537^{xxx}	.596^{xxx}
Extremely or very severe IADL problems	.501^{xxx}	.753^{xxx}
Self-rated health	.001	
Wheelchair	.036	
Severe cognitive impairment	.575^{xxx}	.553^{xxx}
Local supply of nursing home beds	.013^{xxx}	
Income	-.351^{xx}	
Number of surviving children	-.061^{xxx}	-.059^{xx}
Treatment group of basic model	-.086	
Treatment group of 'financial control' model	-0.25	
Constant	-5.853^{xxx}	-5.484

^{x} P <.1 ^{xx} p <.05 ^{xxx} p <.005

Sample size: 427.   Person months: 25449.

substantial probability of admission, assuming that they subscribed to the value that the principal aim was to prevent admission if at all possible. Indeed, they would focus their attention on those at substantial risk of preventable admission, not those with the highest risk of admission, since they would probably be less likely to be successful among the latter. Therefore, the residual value for the case at the first decile of the distribution of predicted probabilities was taken as the criterion.

Were sites with lower caseloads more successful?

Figure 8.2 presents the evidence about the effects of variations in case management inputs between sites on the probabilities of admission to nursing homes.

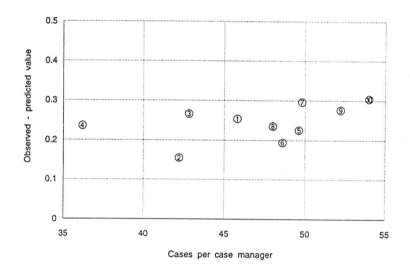

Key to sites

1 Miami	6 Middlesex County
2 Eastern Kentucky	7 Rensselaar County
3 Southern Maine	8 Cleveland
4 Baltimore	9 Philadelphia
5 Greater Lynn	10 Houston

Mean Deviation =   -0.125 + (0.026 x Baltimore/Miami) + (0.001 x Caseload)
Standard Error: {0.012} {0.003}   {0.00025}
R^2 = 0.88   sigF = 0.0002

Average channelling site caseload and mean deviation between actual admissions and probabilities of admission at the 90th percentile of the probability ditribution.

Figure 8.2 Nursing home admission and caseload size for channelling sites

The hypothesis suggested by Figure 8.1 is that the more successful sites would have higher average case management inputs. The criterion of success taken was the difference between outcome and the estimated probability for the first decile case in the site. That is an inverse indicator of success. Case management case-loads is an inverse indicator of case management input per case. Therefore, there would be a positive correlation between the difference and case load size. However, in Baltimore and Miami, assessment tasks were performed by some people, and the remaining case management tasks were performed by others. It is generally argued that case management works best with continuity in case management responsibility. Case management theory stresses the interdependence of assessment and care planning, assessment as a continually repeated – if not continuous – process (Challis *et al.* 1990, Figure 2.1.; Davies,1992, inset 1). Therefore, the regression model test of the hypothesis incorporated site case management case loads and a dummy variable denoting either Baltimore or Miami as well as case load as predictors. The predictions were strongly supported by the model, which fitted well and yielded high significance for each coefficient. The results are summarized in Figure 8.2. Clearly, our hypothesis cannot be rejected.

Within-Site Testing and Estimation

It was not possible to provide within-site tests of the hypothesis from that which the channelling data set because its data did not tie the use of time by case managers to individual cases. However, that has been done in all the PSSRU community care evaluations.

Analyses of the Sheppey and Tonbridge programmes of Thanet-style budget-devolved care management evaluated by John Chesterman and Bleddyn Davies have shown the following.[7]

1. Given needs-related circumstances, higher levels of case management activity undertaken in response to some types of complexity reduced the costs of home care inputs in the Sheppey programme more than others. The analysis distinguished case complexity due to the level of transactional activity (reflected, for instance, in the number of visitors to a case from statutory agencies and in touch with the case manager); complexity due to volatility and change in the needs-related circumstances of clients; and complexity due to relational and attitudinal factors (for instance, ambivalences in the network of informal supporters). Modelling to test and estimate the impact of case management costs on the other home care costs of outputs showed that variations in case management inputs not only had direct effects

---

7   The Sheppey evaluation was of a routine implementation of the original Kent (Thanet) Community Care Project implemented during the late 1970s (Challis and Davies 1986; Davies and Challis 1986; Qureshi, Challis and Davies 1989).

on outcomes, but also indirect effects. In contrast, the effects seemed to be almost entirely direct in the Tonbridge programme.[8]

2. How case management inputs worked to reduce other home care costs becomes clearer when one distinguishes periods in the case-managed career of the cases. By drawing on various kinds of evidence for each case, we were able to distinguish four periods of the case-managed career: a setting-up period (which varied greatly between cases); a continuing care period; a closure period (at the beginning of which it was becoming clear that home care could not be long maintained) and an institutional trial period. We were able to examine weekly and total costs of case management and other home care within each of the periods.

What turned out to be crucial for an understanding of the economics of case-managed community care were:

1. the great differences in the duration of the setting up period (no surprise, because it was a feature of the results of the Thanet project)

2. the extraordinary volatility and change through time in case management and other home care inputs during the continuing care period.

The modelling of individual change for Sheppey is illustrated in Table 8.2; it is exactly what was hypothesized in the protocol for the Kent Community Care project and reasserted in the Thanet books.[9] Case managers with the time to cope with the needs for investments during the setting-up period and subsequently with the extraordinary changes in need-related circumstances can be much more effective in reducing the costs of outcomes in terms of other home care inputs. Responded to flexibly, as in the Sheppey programme, changes for some reduce costs, and for others they increase costs. Indeed, the budgetary consequences of cost-raising changes in total offset the budgetary consequences of the cost-reducing changes, as is illustrated in Figure 8.3.

---

8   The technique used was 2SLS.
9   See, for instance, Davies and Challis (1986), Table 1.1. The argument of the protocol, 'Matching Resources to Needs in Community Care, and Case Management, Equity and Efficiency: The International Experience' was about the circumstances for whom intensive case management would yield the greatest direct and indirect effects. It was one more round in the eternal struggle in which public bureaucracies (such as local authorities) tend always to provide standard packages of inflexible services to 'service recipients' by making the starting assumption that the differences and not the similarities are what is significant about user circumstances for equity and efficiency.

Table 8.2 Rates of Change in Case Management and Other Home Care Costs during the COCA Period in Sheppey*

Rates of change (per cent per annum)	Cmc	Ohcc
-15 or more	0	3
-10 and less than -15	6	6
-5 and less than -10	13	3
-2 and less than -5	9	13
0.01 and less than -2	16	19
0	22	13
0.01 and less than 2	9	9
2 and less than 5	16	13
5 and less than 10	3	6
10 and less than 15	3	6
15 per cent or more	0	9

*Rates of change were estimated arithmetically for cases with only 3 or 4 observations. Growth rates were counted as zero for cases with only 1 or 2 observations.

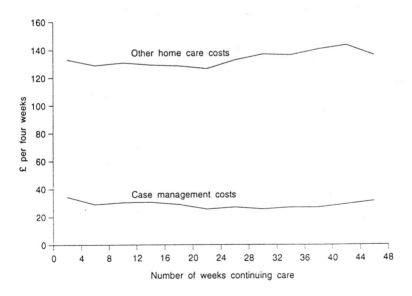

Figure 8.3 COCA case management costs and other home care costs in Sheppey by four-week period (seventeen cases which received continuous support without prolonged institutional stays during 48 weeks in the evaluation year)

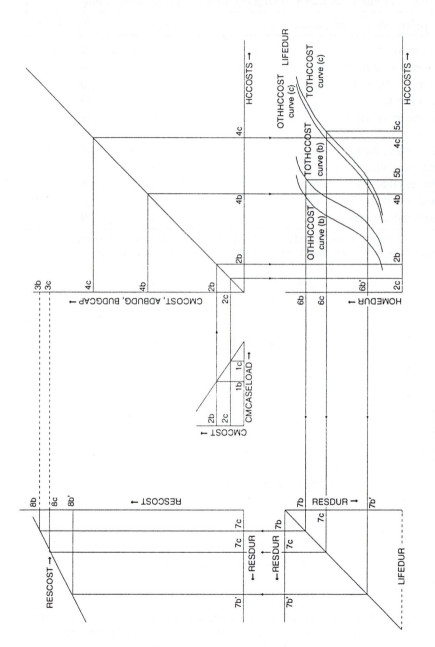

Figure 8.4 Cost relationships and case management perameters: setting perameters to achieve an equitable and efficient balance of care

The high rates of change are of great practical importance for case management arrangements and parameters. What Figure 8.3 suggests is that the relatively flat curves are the bed of a Vesuvian crater. Beneath the surface are upflows and downflows of enormous power and significance for the success of care management. Standing on that surface is always uncomfortable and potentially dangerous, even when the upflows and downflows are broadly in equilibrium. When they are not, disaster is likely: a calamity for the cases, a Pompeiian inundation after which the inadequate feedback system has left the organization almost unaccountable. So the patterns show the importance of being able to respond quickly and flexibly, and so, for instance, of monitoring events to allow quick adjustments of the budgets to which case managers work. Likewise, it illustrates the importance of setting the guidelines and providing correct and fast up-dated information of the type to make a reality of the parameter-setting and adjustment required to make a reality of the kind of model of adjustment illustrated in Figure 8.4. It would then be possible to operate a model in which budget caps and average budgets are set in ways which give the best balance between care-managed home care and its alternatives given the supply curves of alternatives to home care, the relationships of Figure 8.1, and the case mix. The model was developed in Davies, Bebbington, Charnley and colleagues (1990) and used further in Davies (1992). Figure 8.4 provides the cross-references to those arguments.

Discussion

The findings confirm some old messages: care-managed community care can work, particularly care management in which the field workers have the time and skills and sufficiently control the budgets to manage care flexibly and resourcefully. It is vital to target and triage case management – to fit the case management arrangements and parameters to the circumstances of whichever users are targeted on the one hand and local system circumstances on the other – just as it is important for the case managers to do the same with the other resources. Evidence from England, Wales and Scotland collected by many members of the British Society of Gerontology is illustrating how mechanistically relabelling old practices 'case management', and pretending that cosmetic changes to old structures constitutes an intelligent application of the case management approach, will not yield the important indirect efficiency gains from case management.

What Greene argued from his production function of a case management experiment amounted to this: that the channelling projects achieved worse input mix efficiency and failed to make any improvement in technical efficiency than could have been hoped from the case management argument. One might say more: their efforts to get good case management practice were partly negated by their failure to set appropriate case management arrangements and parameters. The argument was similar in nature, though not in degree, to that from our use of production functions for standard provision before social services departments had heard of the importance of the effectiveness of performance of case management tasks, save that the latter functions allowed us to argue that home care services were bad in their outcome mix efficiencies also (Davies *et al.*1990). What the results of this chapter-based on the channelling data and the Sheppey programme does is to focus our attention still more on creating the arrangements and parameters in which care managers can indeed optimise. For gerontologists, the message is that we have an important task of producing the grounded theory for matching case management arrangements and parameters to the circumstances of both the individuals involved and practitioners applying the theory.

References

Applebaum, R.A. and Austin, C.D. (1989) *Long-Term Care Case Management*. New York: Springer.

Applebaum, R. and Austin, C. (1990) *Long Term Care Management: Design and Evaluation*. New York: Springer.

Carcagno, G.J. Applebaum, R. Christianson, J., Phillips, B., Thornton, C. and Will, J. (1986) *The Evaluation of the National Long-Term Care Demonstration: The Planning and Operational Experience of the Channelling Projects: Volume 1*. Princeton, New Jersey: Mathematica Policy Research, Inc.

Challis, D. and Davies, B.P. (1986) *Case Management in Social and Health Care*. Canterbury: PSSRU, University of Kent at Canterbury.

Challis, D. (1993) 'Implementing case management.' In N. Malin (ed) *Implementing Community Care*. Buckingham: Open University Press.

Challis, D.J., Chessum, R., Chesterman, J., Luckett, R. and Traske, K. (1990) *Case Management in Social and Health Care*. Canterbury: PSSRU, University of Kent at Canterbury.

Davies, B.P. and Challis, D. (1986) *Matching Resources to Needs in Community Care*. Canterbury: PSSRU, University of Kent at Canterbury.

Davies, B.P. (1992) *Case Management, Equity & Efficiency, The International Experience*. Canterbury: PSSRU, University of Kent at Canterbury.

Davies, B.P., Bebbington, A.C., Charnley, H. and Colleagues (1990) *Resources, Needs and Outcomes in Community-based Care: A Comparative Study of the Production of Welfare in Ten Local Authorities in England and Wales*. Aldershot: PSSRU Studies, Avebury, 291–3.

Department of Health, Housing and Community Services, Aged and Community Care Division (1992) *It's Your Choice: National Evaluation of Community Options Projects*. Canberra, Australia: Aged and Community Care Service Development and Evaluation Series No 2, Australian Government Publishing Service.

Goodman, C.C. (1981) *Senior Care Action Network: Case Management Model Project Evaluation*. Long Beach, California: Department of Social Work, California State University.

Greene, V.L., Lovely, M.E., Miller, M.D. and Ondrich, J.I. (1992) *Reducing Nursing Home Use Through Community Long-Term Care: An Optimization Analysis*. Syracuse, New York: The Maxwell School, Syracuse University.

Greene, V., Lovely, M.E. and Ondrich, J.I. (1993) 'The cost-effectiveness of community services in a frail elderly population.' *The Gerontologist 33*, 177–190.

Henderson, J.M. and Quandt, R.E. (1980) *Microeconomic Theory: A Mathematical Approach*. Tokyo, Japan: International Student Edition, McGraw-Hill Kogakusha Ltd.

Howe, A., Ozanne, E. and Selby-Smith, C. (eds) (1992) *Community Care Policy and Practice: New Directions in Australia*. Clayton, Victoria, Australia: Monash University Press, Clayton.

Kanter, J. (1989) 'Clinical case management: definition, principles, components.' *Hospital and Community Psychiatry 40*, 361–368.

Moxley, D. (1989) *The Practice of Case Management*. Newbury Park, California: Sage.

Pilling, D. (1988a) *The Case Management Project: Summary of the Evaluation Report*. London: Department of Systems Science, City University, London.

Qureshi, H., Challis, D. and Davies, B. (1989) *Helpers in Case-Managed Community Care*. Canterbury: PSSRU, University of Kent at Canterbury.

CHAPTER 9

'You wouldn't be interested in my life, I've done nothing'
Care Planning and Life-History Work with Frail Older Women

*John Adams, Joanna Bornat
and Mary Prickett*

Introduction

A continuing care ward might seem a curiously out-dated place in which to carry out research. In recent years such wards became part of the forgotten zone of health care as the new generation of health service managers revised the contract of cradle to grave entitlements and responsibilities. Wards were closed. Since 1988 one in four continuing care beds have been redesignated, and older patients are spending shorter periods of time in hospital (*The Guardian* 1994a, 1994b; Association of Community Health Councils 1990). Between 1970 and 1992 the proportion of NHS-funded residents as a proportion of all people in long-term settings declined from 28 per cent to 12 per cent (Laing 1993). While greater numbers of older people are being discharged from acute wards back into their own homes or into mainly privately run nursing and residential homes, the focus for debate about the quality of continuing care has tended to be outside hospital wards, in 'the community' (Age Concern 1991; Royal College of Nursing 1992; Association of Directors of Social Services 1994; Henwood and Wistow 1994). Historically this might not be viewed as a surprising trend, after all, continuing care wards or 'geriatric' care have never enjoyed a good press (Townsend 1964; Roberts 1970; Meacher 1972; Wells 1980) and there has been recent concern about out-dated buildings, unsuitable furnishings and traditional patterns of highly routinized nursing care (Age Concern 1990; Association of Community Health Councils 1993; Bond 1993). Given this poor reputation, why choose continuing care wards as sites to observe care practice; what could we hope to learn from such a setting that could be relevant for older people living in the new institutions of the mixed economy of care?

The first point to be made is that the philosophy and ethos of continuing care, for better or worse, lives on in many different forms and practices. In the private sector, nursing homes tend to be staffed by people whose training and professional experience was developed within hospital contexts, since all professional nurse training was hospital based. However, sensitively modified, medical models of routinized care fit well with regimes which are heavily cost-focused. Our second reason for focusing on continuing care wards was because we were interested in seeing how well care planning practices developed in nursing matched with practices developed largely in community settings. Our third reason for this choice of focus was rooted in a sense of perversity. The words we quote in our title sum up for us the feelings of a group of patients, predominantly women, who, while experiencing good basic nursing care, have few indicators that their existence is in any sense of value. They demonstrate a lack of what Kitwood and Bredin identify as the three components of well-being: personal worth, agency and control and social confidence (Kitwood and Bredin 1992). If conditions for patients and for staff are so difficult, if this area of provision so neglected, then the significance of any findings and recommendations we might arrive at might be all the greater. We might justifiably feel that we had tested our assumptions to the limit.

Ironically, the period during which we carried out our research may well have been the nadir for continuing care, a point from which it may only, can only, rise. A year later and the climate was beginning to show signs of change. Social services chiefs were beginning to question the shifting of costs from health to social care (Community Care, 15–21 Nov. 1994); the chief executive of the NHS was assuring health service managers that the NHS would be continuing to provide continuing care for the chronically sick (*The Guardian* 1994c); and the Health Service Ombudsman had produced a report which raised uncomfortable questions about automatic discharge into private nursing care in the community (Health Service Commissioner 1994). Although more symptomatic of government policy which is concerned about the unpopularity of the logic of its health service 'reforms' it does appear that the future of continuing care in hospitals is not yet settled.

The Project

The research project took place on two continuing care wards situated in different NHS hospitals within the same Health Authority. Both hospitals were previously workhouses and are remembered as such by older members of the local population. The ward on which the women we interviewed lived is an all-female ward of Nightingale design. The method chosen for this study was action research using the 'technical collaborative' approach, in which the researchers test a specific intervention in the practice setting (Holter and Schwartz-Barcott 1993). This means that we, as researchers, brought our own theoretical framework to the setting, and, with the help of practitioners who worked there, attempted to implement an innovation in clinical practice. The knowledge gained in this way was then to be fed back into the refinement of the theoretical basis of the intervention and into the identification of unforeseen problems associated with its implementation.

Data Collection and Analysis

Once we had obtained the necessary consents to begin the study, baseline measurements were undertaken of the patients on the two wards which were the focus of the study. These were the abbreviated mental test of cognition (Hodkinson, 1972) and the Selfcare (D) rating scale for depression (Black, Knight and Belford 1990). Barthel scores, which indicate the ability to perform activities of daily living, were calculated from information supplied by the nursing staff (Collin et al. 1988). These tests were undertaken in order to establish some of the characteristics of the patient sample. Ward A (the ward where our four case study women lived) accommodated 30 continuing care patients whose mean Barthel score was 3.97 out of a possible 20. Ten patients consented to undertake the cognition test (seven patients' scores indicated impairment) and eight patients agreed to complete the Selfcare (D) (three had scores suggesting depression).

We approached those continuing care patients who were capable of giving consent, to ask if they would be willing to take part in a tape-recorded interview about their lives before admission to the hospital. Nine interviews were conducted on Ward A, using an informal interview technique which aimed to allow respondents to convey their own concerns and priorities when invited to talk about their lives. In addition, two interviews were conducted with the relatives of patients who were unable to be interviewed themselves due to physical or psychological disability. The interviews were then transcribed and a copy of the tape and transcription was given to each patient or relative who had taken part.

Our original 'technical collaborative' research design had included the nurses. Our aim had been to develop a method of life-story book development which was simple, not costly and which did not require a heavy time commitment. Our efforts met with resistance. Nurses were, with only one exception, always 'too busy' to take part, even on a partnership basis with one of the research team. Revising our approach we decided to proceed by demonstrating the process ourselves. Using the biographical information contained in the interview transcripts as a basis, we assembled a life-story book, using a cheap but attractively designed scrapbook, for eleven of the patients. Further discussion of issues raised in the taped interviews followed before the final content of the books was fixed. In some cases, personal photographs were produced and these were copied for inclusion. The local history collection of the public library provided much useful illustrative material and, for images of other parts of the country, tourist information offices proved to be helpful. For some of the books a 'life line' which set the life-story of the individual in the context of the major historical events in a simple graphical form was constructed and for these, and some others where there was sufficient information about a particular life, a genogram was constructed.

Literature Review

The literature relating to reminiscence research and work is now well documented (Haight 1991; Merriam 1980; Bornat 1989). From the first phase of assumptions as to benefits and rewards (Butler 1963; Lewis 1971; Dobrof 1984) debates have moved on through attempts to measure outcomes, test methods and compare responses. Analyses of reminiscence have yielded taxonomies of process, form and content (Coleman 1986; Merriam 1989; Watt and Wong 1991). Discussions of therapeutic value and process abound and are resourced with research and critical evaluation (Thornton and Brotchie 1987; Bornat 1993). Instrumental approaches to the use of biographical information generated through reminiscence-focused interviews have been developed as a means to enhancing the quality of care and support for older people in a range of settings (Cook 1984; Adams 1989; Norris 1989; Fielden 1990; Burnside 1990; Lowenthal and Marazzo 1990; McKenzie 1991; O'Donovan 1993; Dant and Gully 1994).

There is thus a wealth of evidence, much of which is soundly based in detailed research and observation, yet there still appear to us to be assumptions which require closer examination. The initial development of reminiscence and life-history work drew heavily on psychologically based models of fulfilment, life-stage role and therapeutic reward (Erikson 1963; Butler 1963). More recently, researchers from a number of different disciplines have begun to consider the social context of remembering (Boden and Bielby 1986; Wallace 1992; Moody 1988; Buchanan and Middleton 1993). Such accounts draw attention to the function which reminiscence and biographical remembering plays in the lives of older people and some, in particular, emphasize the particular tasks which face older people living in institutional settings (Holland and Rabbitt 1991; Wallace 1992).

A second area where it seemed development was needed was in what we describe as the instrumental use of biography in the care and support of older people (Adams and Bornat 1992). The Open University's Gloucester Project (Johnson *et al.* 1988) has done much to provide a practice based justification and development of biographical assessment and care planning in community settings. Nurses working with patients with dementia have been directed towards approaches which seek to combine biographical details with clinical data (Jones and Miesen 1992; O'Donovan 1993). Both approaches have their limitations: the Gloucester Project presents problems for under-resourced units since it requires the preparation of detailed and lengthy life-histories. The nursing models developed so far err in the other direction, being too heavily itemized and check-list oriented to allow for much personal variability. Both, in our opinion, fail to take into account questions of ownership or access to the documentation, or the need for that documentation to be incorporated into the ongoing care management of the particular individual. In developing this critique we were informed by current thinking on models of social work with older people, being particularly influenced by approaches which stress the importance of counselling, advocacy, self determination and empowerment (Smale, Tuson et al. 1993; Parsloe and Stevenson 1993; Phillipson 1993; Hugman 1994). It was for these reasons that a major focus of the research project became the developments of life-story books for patients.

Creating Life-Story Books

In order to highlight some of the issues raised by the creation of life-story scrapbooks for patients in continuing care wards, we have selected four brief case studies using material drawn from the interviews, the life-story books and our own research diaries:

Barbara Smith

Barbara Smith had been living in the ward for about a year where she had become renowned as the ward character, her bed by the door being the usual stopping off place for visitors. Men in particular were objects of her wit and pointed comments. She had come to the ward after becoming unable to cope alone in her warden-controlled bungalow in a local village. She had been born in that village and had lived there all her life and its people and landmarks formed the basis of her life-story. The nurse leading the care team looking after Mrs Smith also lived in that village and so she took part in the process of creating the life-story book with enthusiasm. She enjoyed extending her knowledge of the village including the part which Mrs Smith had played in its life. The other main feature which Mrs Smith wanted to include in her scrapbook were pictures of the Channel Islands where she had spent many happy holidays with her late husband. Thus far the creation of a scrapbook for her was unproblematic. Potentially difficult issues were raised, however, by the transcript of her interview which contained several pejorative comments about various younger members of her family. This aspect of life-story work raises difficult issues for professional carers, as it might be seen to be providing a permanent medium for potentially libellous material. This caused some consternation amongst the nursing staff who became anxious about issues of ownership and control over the material.

Norma Green

Mrs Green had been living in the ward for the last three and a half years. Her medical problems made communication difficult, but it was usually possible to understand a high proportion of what she said. Her biographical interview revealed that she had led an eventful life which had involved much travel. The aspect of her life to which she always returned, however, was the contrast between 'now' and 'then'. When younger she had gained certificates and won prizes for her stage skills in speech and drama. She was keen to include in her life-story book photographs showing her solo stage performances as celebrated figures from history which she portrayed to great acclaim at local festivals. Similarly, many of the jobs which she had done in her working life had depended upon the skill with which she could use her voice. In view of these past talents, she found it bitterly ironic that her present illness had robbed her of those talents and made any sort of communication difficult. As researchers we felt that the process of highlighting this aspect of Norma Green's past life through the medium of a scrapbook raised difficult issues to do with the stark contrast between the past self and the present one. It was probably no coincidence that her Selfcare (D) suggested that she was suffering from depression.

Laura Black

Mrs Black had been hospitalized for three years and though she had lost the use of the left side of her body following a stroke, her speech and vision were not affected and she was one of the most vocal and articulate members of the ward community. Widowed with two middle-aged children and two grandchildren she had worked in the local industry, the shoe trade, during her youth. Her unmarried daughter lives in the house which Laura and her husband moved into shortly after their marriage. She goes back to her house several times a year, helped by her son, and is able to keep up contact with friends on these occasions by 'phone. She likes to smoke, an activity which she now has few opportunities to enjoy. As non-smoking researchers we were thrown into confusion. We were working in an institution whose anti-smoking policies we were only too pleased to see enforced. Indeed, Laura herself commented that if she had never smoked she would probably not have been in hospital now. When offered a cigarette by the ward sister she said she would like two and clearly enjoyed them as we talked in a side room which had been set aside for her interview. The cigarette became a focus for subversion in which we all colluded though, it should be stressed, the interviewer most unwillingly. As the interview unfolded, Laura described her enjoyment of cigarettes:

> I shouldn't, not that I have a lot, not a lot, not as many as I did when I was at home. 'Cause at home is a big temptation isn't it? After dinner...get on the old settee, paper, newspaper...nod off, then wake up and think, Oh God, it's time for a cup of tea, you know, and carry on like that.

Perhaps she was treating the interview as a moment for 'off the record' reflection and relaxation. An interesting contrast between the formal process of the interview as perceived by the interviewer and the 'informality' she was giving us access to.[1]

Caroline White

Miss White had been in hospital for seven years. She had lost the use of the right side of her body and was unable to focus her eyes to read or watch television. She frequently had difficulty in putting into words what she wanted to say. Perhaps because of this she preferred not to join the other patients in the day-room although it was not altogether clear whether or not this was really her choice. Miss White never married and was an only child. Her surviving relatives were cousins who visited her regularly but for whom she expressed some resentment due to the way she says they disposed of her property. When she was admitted to hospital her landlord sought to get her house cleared and, as a result, all her possessions, including virtually all her family photographs were thrown away. She was a quiet, withdrawn and isolated woman who seemed at first unable to communicate at all. She was initially unwilling to take part in the full research project but became drawn in when one of the team began to talk to her about her earlier life. Attention from the interviewer showed that Miss White did indeed enjoy talking and could describe aspects of her past life. What developed was more like a conversation than a formal interview and provided her with an opportunity for quiet intimacy and opportunities to communicate her discontent with her present situation and enjoy her favourite sweets with one of the research team. She chose to tell a life-story, though as a representation of an identity it seemed somewhat incomplete. She elaborated on the good relationship she had enjoyed with her mother, but seemed not to have much to say about her father and was not expansive on the subject of marriage: 'Never thought about it, never really looked at anybody either'. However, what did emerge was her love of animals. She had enjoyed the company of animals through-out her life up to her admission to hospital and references cropped up again and again during her interviews: 'I like them all, if I could've had a good, if I'd had some money and I could've bought a house in a big field with animals, I could have had all animals to look after, but I hadn't got it, so I couldn't do it'.

Discussion

In what follows we review the experience of creating life-story books and identify four issues: complexity, integration, appropriateness and identity construction.

---

1   We are grateful to Pam Shakespeare for this smoker's eye perspective

Complexity

The benefits of a 'memory diary' in improving communication between patients, their relatives and nurses have been emphasized (O'Donovan 1993) and our experience showed many occasions when this was so. However, it must not be assumed, despite the many assumptions which abound in the literature of reminiscence practice (McKenzie 1991; Osborn 1993) that all biographical accounts will reflect contentment, acceptance and family harmony.

Our action research project indicated a need to establish agreed protocols in order to minimise difficulties which could arise if life-story books are to be widely used in institutional settings. The women we worked with were keen to have their life-story books accessibly displayed near to them. We supported them in this choice since it was our aim that the material should help to inform decisions about their care planning. And it was in fact at this stage that we found members of the nursing staff beginning to show a keen interest in what we had achieved. However, open display on bedside cupboards or on bed-ends (there was very little personal or private space available to these patients) raises problems if contentious material becomes available for general consumption. Issues to be addressed include the question of whether boundaries need to be established around the material to be included in discussion with the life-story author, particularly if that material includes negative comments about people who are still alive. Also, what should happen to the material after a patient dies? Barbara Smith prided herself on speaking her mind and was known to hold less than complimentary opinions about several members of her family. When she died, her family requested a copy of her tape-recorded interview and its transcript – which she had chosen not to show them. In this case it transpired that the tape contained little or nothing offensive to her family, but it alerted us to an issue which needs to be addressed in biographical work: the complexity of accounts.

Integration

If biographical approaches to care planning are to be widely adopted, they must be fully integrated into the philosophy and patient management systems of the clinical area. Our project did not have the resources to explore in a systematic way the differences which could be made to the delivery of care, but our observations led us to consider some of the issues involved.

Both the wards in our study used a model of nursing derived from Roper, Logan and Tierney, which provides a list of twelve activities of living. They state that the focus of nursing: 'is not on needs but on the activities of living because they are the observable behavioural manifestations of basic human needs' (Roper, Logan and Tierney 1983). Reed and Robbins (1991) have argued that this focus on the observable and measurable may be more appropriate to acute care settings than to long term ones. Also 'problem-solving' may not be realistic for many of the problems which have been identified. This prioritization seems to derive from the commonly-used diagram of Maslow's 'hierarchy of needs' as a pyramid with physiological needs taking precedence over and dwarfing, psycho-social ones (Kenworthy, Snowley and Gilling 1992, p.57). However, Adair (1990) has argued that Maslow never presented his theory of human needs in this form, and that it would be more appropriate to present it as a series of boxes of ascending size. This very different description suggests that while physical needs may have to be met first, other needs may be far greater. Our experience in creating life-story books with our four case study individuals leads us to suggest that this revised interpretation of Maslow's hierarchy is likely to be a more appropriate representation of the requirements on a continuing care ward.

Norma Green has multiple physiological problems leading to a heavy dependency on nursing care. Her physical dependency caused her much sorrow and regret. However, she was able to take an active part in developing a life-story book, selecting images and describing many fulfilling aspects of earlier phases of her life. Though her basic physiological needs could be met on a daily basis through established nursing routines, her need to be identified as someone who had lived a richly varied life and who was still able to reflect and discuss her life-story in positive terms, despite signs of depression, suggests that such activities should be included as part of the provision of care which enters an individual's care plan. It is interesting that her response to an opportunity to present her life-story shows her cutting across two of the categories identified by Coleman in his longitudinal study of reminiscence processes (Coleman 1986, p.37). She has low morale yet she values her memories of the past though they do raise hurtful ironies in their contrast with her present state. People in her situation have psycho-social needs which biographical work can help to identify and support if developed in a way which gives the individual opportunities to present and display a life.

Appropriateness

Laura Black's interview, as we suggested in the case study, was one for which she, in various informal ways, controlled the conditions despite her outwardly powerless state. Reflecting on the experience has led us to emphasize the distinction between life review and simple reminiscing drawn by Coleman and Merriam. Both look for ways to distinguish unembellished 'recall of past experiences' (Merriam 1989) from a process of 'applying the past to the present by the expression of relevant information derived from the past' (Coleman 1974). Haight also emphasizes the difference between the two, stressing the 'integrative' function of life review (Haight 1988). The reminiscence literature contains many references to ways in which late-life remembering can help to resolve conflicts and promote a feeling of fulfillment and recognition (Bornat 1989; Gibson 1993; Bender 1993; Coleman 1993). Yet expectations that the two may be combined in continuing care settings through use of publicly available life-story books may be unrealistic. Laura Black's interview provides an insight into the way in which this distinction may be appropriately managed by the interviewee.

When talking about the circumstances of her birth and childhood, Laura would occasionally whisper and although she provided an account, was not willing for this to be included in her life-story book. This distinction between a private and a public account is perhaps another way to distinguish simple reminiscing from life review. She connected this early part of her life with a later stage, explaining how her particular responsibilities for caring for her mother stemmed from the circumstances of her birth and parentage. Nevertheless, she was determined to keep this account within a private sphere of communication.

Laura's interview provided an opportunity for her to explain her life to someone who was not part of her daily public life within an institutional setting. However, what could have led to a thought-provoking insight into changing social attitudes was not to be related outside the interview (and indeed in describing this issue we have attempted not to breach a confidence). This suggests that for Laura, and for others, reminiscence in a collective care setting may well be an edited version of a life and one which may be chosen with a sense of appropriateness and convention. To say 'I've done nothing' may thus be a necessary protection for a woman who now lives a public life but who is still able to establish areas of privacy around her identity. Consequently, the contribution which her life-story book makes to her care planning needs to be viewed as her edited version and the one which she feels is appropriate to her care needs in her present environment.

Individualization

The development of a life-story book drawing on Caroline White's interview transcripts appeared at first sight to present something of a challenge. It seemed that there would be little to include. Because of her communication difficulties and the fact that she had only two or three surviving family photographs the basic elements normally considered essential in the construction of an identity and which others could also comprehend, were few. Her experience matches those of people who have lived the greater part of their life in institutions (Atkinson 1993). In the end, she seemed to be pleased with the suggestion that we include images of animals resembling those she had described, which we cut out of magazines. Though the nurses responded well to her book and she was evidently pleased with it, always making sure that it was available for people to see, the identity she presented was one which was more of a starting point than any completed description of conventional milestones through life.

If uninterpreted or decontextualized, her life-story book could serve to confirm the stereotype which appeared to have been applied to her on the ward: a passive person with limited powers of reflection. Descriptions of domestic animals, however lovingly remembered, are not, at face value, particularly illuminating of social place or life experience. What is needed instead is an appreciation of the identity which Miss White offers now, as a patient on a continuing care ward facing major problems of individualization. With time and commitment, her interest in animals could become a key to other aspects of her life. She had given us a way to engage with her feelings and the meaningful times she has experienced. Further interviews and conversations could thus help her to produce more of herself. There is potential to work up a more individualized and elaborated projection of her identity.

We make this final point as a response and caution to those approaches which appear to us to be built around the abilities of older people to actively present themselves as distinctive individuals, either through narrative skill, or through the sheer uniqueness of their life story (O'Donovan 1993; Thompson 1989). If life-story books are to play a part in care planning then such a presentation as Caroline White's inevitably presents a challenge to carers and requires us to view the process as one of ongoing development and elaboration rather than as a finished account.

Conclusions

Our study did not provide any evidence of physical care needs identified through the process of biographical interviewing which had been missed by the existing system of nursing assessment. This suggests that approaches derived from Roper, Logan and Tierney's activities of living are effective and should be retained (Roper, Logan and Tierney 1983). However, the adoption of Adair's presentation of Maslow's scheme of needs would indicate that the existing approach to assessment represents the beginning rather than the end of the process (Adair 1990). The collection of biographical information and its presentation in the form of a life-story book provides a framework which encourages the development of knowledge about the person who risks being obscured by the diagnoses. We have much anecdotal evidence that through the process of creating such books, nursing staff gained new insights into the previous life experiences, tastes, and significant relationships of patients for whom they had often been providing care for long periods of time. Our experience accords with Baines, Saxby and Ehlert's study of care staff and residents in a residential home which found that before the experimental interventions were undertaken, the staff only knew an average of 5.33 out of a possible 40 biographical items about each resident (Baines, Saxby and Ehlert 1987). It seems that proximity and the passage of time does not inevitably result in the acquisition of the biographical information which could form the basis of a therapeutic relationship between resident and carer.

The value of this approach has been well summarized in reports of the Gloucester Project (Boulton *et al*. 1988), where there is a focus on the importance of life-stories as a source of alternative and more individually meaningful accounts in contrast to those elicited through traditional assessment techniques, their contribution to self esteem amongst older people and the the importance of earlier life experiences and the relationships and activities which continue to be of significance when coping with loss in later life.

The challenge for nursing is to devise the means to incorporate biographical information into the working knowledge of carers in such a way that the uniqueness of the individual is preserved. The traditional check-list approach cannot hope to do justice to the complexity of the life-story which many people want to communicate, but the decision to go beyond makes new demands on nurses. They must be prepared to be open to the expression of anger, depression, jealousy, regret and guilt as well as to more attractive emotions such as acceptance, cheerfulness and nostalgia. If life-story books are to play their part in care planning, as we suggest they should, this also needs to be accompanied by a degree of realism and reservation. The complexity of the story told, the need to seek ways for continuing integration and development of the story and the importance of focusing on the patient's right to identify what is appropriate as she seeks her own route to individualization have all to be recognized.

The nursing profession must also look again at the purpose and scope of care planning. While the United Kingdom Central Council for Nursing, Midwifery and Health Visiting's publication, 'Standards for Records and Record Keeping' (UKCC 1993) includes the welcome requirement that nursing documentation should: '...include a record of any factors (physical, psychological or social) that appear to affect the patient or client...' the one article which refers specifically to 'situations where the condition of the patient or client is apparently unchanging' (24) is concerned solely with the need to establish local policies on the maximum time that is allowed to elapse between entries. Clearly, nurses have a legal responsibility to document the care which they assess, plan and implement, but it would be unfortunate if legal requirements came to dominate the philosophy of care planning. For as long as the care plan is held to define the legitimate scope of nursing intervention, the lack of a biographical dimension to the process of establishing a care plan greatly reduces the liklihood that the transmission of such knowledge will occur. We look forward to the development of new conceptual tools which will make the unification of physical and psycho-social elements in care planning. We offer our experience in developing life-story books as a contribution to the emergence of such an approach in the nursing care of older people in continuing care.

References

Adair J. (1990) *Understanding Motivation*. Guildford: Talbot Adair Press.

Adams, J. (1989) 'Anamnesis in dementia: restoring a personal history.' *Oral History 17*, 2, 62–63.

Adams, J. and Bornat, J. (1992) 'Models of biography and reminiscence in the nursing care of frail elderly people.' In J.M. Via and E. Portella (eds) *Volume II of the Proceedings of the 4th International Conference on Systems Science in Health-Social Services for the Elderly and the Disabled*. Barcelona: Fundacion de Barcelona.

Age Concern England (1990) *Under Sentence: Continuing Care Accommodation for Older People Within the National Health Service: A Discussion Paper*. London: Age Concern.

Age Concern England (1991) *Dis-continuing Care: Report of a Survey of District Health Authority Plans for Continuing Care of Elderly People*. London: Age Concern.

Association of Community Health Councils (1990) *NHS Continuing Care of Elderly People*. London: ACHC.

Association of Directors of Social Services (1994) *Continuing Care: Continuing Concern*. Stockport: ADSS.

Atkinson, D. (1993) 'I got put away: group-based reminiscence with people with learning difficulties.' In J. Bornat *Reminiscence Reviewed: Perspectives, Evaluations, Achievements*. Buckingham: Open University Press.

Baines, S., Saxby, P. and Ehlert, K. (1987) 'Reality orientation and reminiscence therapy: a controlled cross-over study of elderly confused people.' *British Journal of Psychiatry 151*, 222–231.

Bender, M. (1993) 'An interesting confusion: what can we do with reminiscence groupwork.' In J. Bornat (ed) *Reminiscence Reviewed: Evaluations, Achievements, Perspectives*. Buckingham: Open University Press.

Black, J., Knight, P. and Belford, H. (1990) 'The use of selfcare (D) rating scale for depression in elderly continuing care patients – a pilot study.' *Care of the Elderly 2*, 3, 119–121.

Boden, D. and Bielby, D. (1983) 'The past as resource: a conversational analysis of elderly talk.' *Human Development 26*, 208–319.

Bond, J. (1993) 'Living arrangements of elderly people.' In J. Bond, P. Coleman and S. Peace (eds) *Ageing in Society: An Introduction to Social Gerontology*, 2nd edition. London: Sage.

Bornat, J. (1989) 'Oral history as a social movement: reminiscence and older people.' *Oral History 17*, 2, 16–24.

Bornat, J. (1993) (ed) *Reminiscence Reviewed: Evaluations, Achievements, Perspectives*. Buckingham: Open University Press.

Boulton, J., Gully, V., Matthews, L. and Gearing, B. (1988) *Developing the Biographical Approach in Practice with Older People*. Buckingham: The Open University and Policy Studies Institute.

Buchanan, K. and Middleton, D. (1993) 'Reminiscence reviewed: a discourse analytic perspective.' In J. Bornat (ed) *Reminiscence Reviewed: Achievements, Evaluations, Perspectives*. Buckingham: Open University Press.

Burnside, I. (1990) 'Reminiscence: an independent nursing intervention in the aged.' *Issues in Mental Health Nursing 11*, 38–48.

Butler, R.N. (1963) 'The life review: an interpretation of reminiscence in the aged.' *Psychiatry 26*, 65–73.

Coleman, P. (1974) 'Measuring reminiscence characteristics from conversations as adaptive features of old age.' *International Journal of Aging and Human Development 5*, 281–294.

Coleman, P. (1986) *Ageing and Reminiscence Process*. Chichester: Wiley.

Coleman, P. (1993) 'Reminiscence within the study of aging.' In J. Bornat (ed) *reminiscence Reviewed: Perspective, Evaluations, Achievements ts*. Buckingham: Open University Press.

Community Care (1994) 'Draft Dodging.' 15–21 November.

Collin, C., Wade, D.T., Davies, S. and Horne, V. (1988) 'The Barthel ADL index: a reliability study.' *International Disability Studies 10*, 61–63.

Cook, J.R. (1984) 'Reminiscing: how it can help confused nursing home resident.' *Social Casework 65*, 2, 90–93.

Dant, T. and Gully, V. (1994) *Coordinating Care at Home*. London: Collins.

Dobrof, R. (1984) 'Introduction; a time for reclaiming the past.' *Journal of Gerontological Social Work 7*, 1/2, xvii–xix.

Erikson, E.H. (1963) *Childhood and Society*. New York: Norton.

Fielden, M. (1990) 'Reminiscence as a therapeutic intervention with sheltered housing residents: a comparative study.' *British Journal of Social Work 20*, 21–44.

Gibson, F. (1993) 'What can reminiscence contribute to people with dementia?' In J. Bornat (ed) *Reminiscence Reviewed: Evaluations, Developments, Perspectives*. Buckingham: Open University Press.

The Guardian (1994a) New NHS guidelines may make elderly pay for care. 8 July.

The Guardian (1994b) Those who must pay the price of growing old. 3 September.

The Guardian (1994c) Excessive cuts in care for ill old people will be restored. 18 November.

Haight, B. (1988) 'The theraputic role of a structured life review process in homebound elderly subjects.' *Journal of Gerontology 43*, 2, p.40–44.

Haight, B. (1991) 'Reminiscing: the state of the art as a basis for practice.' *International Journal of Aging and Human Development 33*, 1, 1–32.

Health Service Commissioner (1994) *Failure to Provide Long Term NHS Care for a Brain-Damaged Patient*; Second Report for Session 1993–4. London: HMSO.

Henwood, M. and Wistow, G. (1994) *Hospital Discharge and Community Care: Early Days*. Leeds: Nuffield Institute for Health, Community Care Division.

Hodkinson, H.M. (1972) 'Evaluation of a mental test score for assessment of mental impairment in the elderly.' *Age and Ageing 1*, 233–238.

Holland, C. and Rabbitt, P. (1991) 'Ageing memory: use versus impairment.' *British Journal of Psychology 82*, 29–38.

Holter, I.M. and Schwartz-Barcott, D. (1993) 'Action research: what is it? How has it been used and how can it be used in nursing?' *Journal of Advanced Nursing 18*, 298–304.

Hugman, R. (1994) 'Social work and case management in the UK: models of professionalism and elderly people.' *Ageing and Society 14*, 2, 237–253.

Jones, G. and Miesen, B. (1992) (eds) *Care-giving in Dementia: Research and Applicationist*. London: Tavistock.

Johnson, M., Gearing, B., Carley, M. and Dant, T. (1988) A bibliographicallly based health and social diagnostic technique: a research report. Project Paper No.4. Milton Keynes: Open University and Policy Studies Institute.

Kenworthy, N., Snowley, G. and Gilling, C. (1992) (eds) *Common Foundation Studies in Nursing*. Edinburgh: Churchill Livingstone.

Kitwood, T. and Bredin, K. (1992) 'Towards a theory of dementia care: personhood and well-being.' *Ageing and Society 12*, 3, 269–287.

Laing, W. (1993) *Laing's Review of Private Health Care*. London: Laing and Buisson.

Lewis, C.N. (1971) 'Reminiscing and self-concept in old age.' *Journal of Gerontology 26*, 240–242.

Lowenthal, R.I. and Marrazzo, R.A. (1990) 'Milestoning: evoking memories for resocializig through group reminiscence.' *The Gerontologist 30*, 2, 269–272.

McKenzie, S. (1991) 'A positive force.' *Nursing the Elderly 3*, 3, May/June, 22–24.

Meacher, M. (1972) *Taken for a Ride: Special Homes for Confused Old People*. London: Longman.

Merriam, S.B. (1980) 'The concept and function of reminiscence: a review of research.' *The Gerontologist 20*, 604–609.

Merriam, S.B. (1989) 'The structure of simple reminiscence.' *The Gerontolgist 29*, 6, 761–767.

Moody, H.R. (1988) 'Twenty-five years of the life review: where did we come from? Where are we going?' *Journal of Gerontological Social Work 12*, 2/4, 7–21.

Norris, A. (1989) 'Clinic or client? a psychologist's case for reminiscence.' *Oral History 17*, 2, 26–29.

O'Donovan, S. (1993) 'The memory lingers on.' *Elderly Care 5*, 1, Jan/Feb, 27–31.

Osborn, C. (1993) *The Reminiscence Handbook*. London: Age Exchange.

Parsole, P. and Stevenson, O. (1993) 'A powerhouse for change: empowering users.' In J. Johnson and R. Slater (eds) *Ageing and Later Life*. London: Sage.

Phillipson, C. (1993) 'Approaches to advocacy.' In J. Johnson and R. Slater (eds) *Ageing and Later Life*. London: Sage.

Reed, J. and Robbins, I. (1991) 'Models of nursing: their relevance to the care of elderly people.' *Journal of Advanced Nursing 16*, 1350–1357.

Roberts, N. (1970) *Our Future Selves*. London: George Allen and Unwin.

Roper, N., Logan, W.W. and Tierney, A. (1983) *Using a Model for Nursing*. Edinburgh: Churchill Livingstone.

Royal College of Nursing (1992) *A Scandal Waiting to Happen? Elderly People and Nursing Care in Residential and Nursing Homes*. London: RCN.

Smale, G., Tuson, G. *et al*. (1993) *Empowerment, Assessment, Care Management and the Skilled Worker*. London: National Institute for Social Work/HMSO.

Thompson, A. (1989) 'Times past.' *Nursing Times 85*, 6, 31–32.

Thornton, S. and Brotchie, J. (1987) 'Reminiscence: a critical review of the empirical literature.' *British Journal of Clinical Psychology 26*, 93–111.

Townsend, P. (1964) *The Last Refuge*. London: Routledge and Kegan Paul.

UKCC (1993) *Standards for Records and Record Keeping*. London: United Kingdom Central Council for Nursing, Midwifery and Health Visiting.

Wallace, B.J. (1992) 'Reconsidering the life review: the social construction of talk about the past.' *The Gerontologist 21*, 1, 120–125.

Watt, L.M. and Wong, P.T.P. (1991) 'A taxonomy of reminiscence and therapeutic implications.' *Journal of Gerontologial Social Work 16*, 1/2, 37–57.

Wells, T.J. (1980) *Problems in Geriatic Nursing Care*. Edinburgh: Churchill Livingstone.

CHAPTER 10

Ethnicity and Care Management

Elaine Cameron, Frances Badger
and Helen Evers

'...there's only so much to go around. I'm not hungry, I've got a house,
you have to queue...you get there in the end'

Jamaican man talking about services
(Cameron, Evers and Badger 1993)

Introduction

Community care involves a commitment to the development of user-centred, needs-led and equitable services. Indeed, local authorities are obliged
to consult with all sections of the community and to give users and carers a
central role in decisions about their own care plans. However, these obligations often prove difficult for services to achieve in practice, and all too often
the reasons are given as inadequate funds and resources.

This chapter argues that the reality is far more complex. Many service
providers are unaware of the many ways in which they are failing to meet
their commitments for some groups of people in the community, such as
ethnic minorities. Resource levels are important, but only part of the picture.
Proper consideration of ethnicity, along with other social factors such as
class, gender and age, is central to efforts to achieve the goals of community
care. Our research indicates that services can make significant progress
towards meeting some of the goals of community care for disadvantaged
groups.

In this chapter we focus on ethnicity in relation to two important aspects
of care management: equitable services and needs-led assessment. We draw
on our recent research into the needs of and services for old Asian and black
people in Wolverhampton (Cameron, Evers and Badger 1993). This study,
commissioned by Social Services and the Health Authority, focused on the
views, stories and experiences of old people and their carers and families as
well as the perspectives of service providers. We were able to look at 'needs',
care management and service responses, therefore, in the widest possible
way. An 'action' orientation kept practical considerations well to the fore, so

we were able to suggest criteria for service 'good practice' as well as options for service development in policy and practice.

The terms we use here to describe people's ethnic origin varies according to sources and context. In the main they follow the definitions from our research which used the terms which people used to describe themselves:

- *Afro-Caribbean*
  General term used to denote a person who identifies with or has roots in the West Indies or Africa. Includes people who are 'Jamaican', 'black', 'West Indian' or 'black British'. Other terms in current usage having the same referent include 'black African', 'black Caribbean and 'African Caribbean'.

- *Asian*
  General term used to denote a person who identifies with or has roots in the Indian sub-continent. Includes people who identify with or originate from East Africa.

- *Black*
  General term used to denote a person who identifies with or is of Afro-Caribbean origin'

- *Culture*
  General term referring broadly to a way of life: distinctive social institutions...social norms, manners, attitudes and ways of thinking, diet, dress.

- *Ethnicity*
  Refers to a sharing of perceptions of 'peoplehood', language, religion and culture as a basis for personal and group identity.

- *Race*
  Perceived physical qualities of a person, e.g. skin colour that may serve to differentiate between individuals or groups of people.

(Cameron, Evers and Badger 1993,
following Blakemore and Boneham 1994)

Clearly there are important and relevant debates about terminology to address here, but we refer the reader to a useful discussion of concepts in Blakemore and Boneham (1994), which informed our thinking.

Whilst our approach in this discussion is to follow the philosophy of community care and 'put people first', we nevertheless find it useful to consider the political and historical legacies that continue to have an impact on the way services are organized and function. This will give a brief indication of the context within which services now operate. It will point to some of the long-standing organizational and professional imperatives that contribute to the challenges services now face with regard to equitable provision and needs-led assessment.

Why should people with an interest in care management be specially concerned about black and minority ethnic groups? The demographic picture shows that black and Asian people, – by far the largest ethnic minority groups – currently comprise about 4 per cent of the population. However, they are not distributed evenly. For example in some wards of Wolverhampton, more than 40 per cent of the population is of Asian or Afro-Caribbean origin. This uneven distribution reflects the history of migration and settlement (see Blakemore and Boneham 1994). But population figures are not the only reason why we should be interested. Community care policy is about equitable treatment: without a focus on black and minority ethnic groups, this cannot possibly be achieved.

Policy on Service Provision and its Organizational Context

In this section, we identify some key features:

- Policy with regard to ethnicity has tended to remain largely undeveloped; generally there has been only a slow incorporation of the reality of a multi-racial Britain.

- Where policy makers and services have addressed multi-racial issues, they have tended to focus on cultural diversity, seeing 'need' as stemming from culture. The cause of the 'problem' or 'need' therefore, is seen to be rooted in culture rather than other social or economic factors such as poverty or bad housing.

- Services have tended to remain ethnocentric. Generally speaking, information and monitoring systems have not been in place to enable services to evaluate what they provide or do for people. Additionally, little systematic or appropriate information has been available about local ethnic minority groups or their perspectives on their needs.

- 'One service for all' tends to be the base-line philosophy underpinning notions of equal opportunities within services. Where there have been initiatives in providing 'ethnically sensitive' services, these have often been 'bolted on' to existing provision, where users are seen as having 'special' needs. Services thereby often simply replace old stereotypes with new ones.

- Service providers have generally had few opportunities to acquire appropriate professional skills to meet the challenges of multi-racial care management. Terms such as 'race', ethnicity and culture tend to be used in confused and unclear ways. The traditional emphasis of services on service-based categories and client groups diverts attention away from commonalities between peoples from minority ethnic groups and others, for example in old age or among women.

There is, of course, enormous diversity among people from ethnic minority groups; Asian and black people may be the majority group in a community. Ethnicity is not always the main focus for people's own identity, yet ethnicity is often over-used as an 'explanatory' factor for problems and for needs.

- Racism in wider society continues to be reflected in the organization and operation of services.

Following on from this, a critical view might suggest that community care spells further disadvantage for people from ethnic minority groups. There are a number of reasons why this should be the case: the ideology of community care, by seeming to take account of an individual's personal situation, is masking and exacerbating existing inequalities in care; the shift in policy is really only a means to ration scarce service resources. Some local authorities are currently facing major problems as funds run out. Any changes to services are usually only superficial and cosmetic, so that services remain largely ethnocentric especially in crucial areas, e.g. needs assessment, service development and both the array and the provision of services on offer; there has been little real shift in terms of empowerment of users and carers; the increasing importance of the voluntary sector, with its problems of continuity and funding means less than satisfactory mainstream service provision and further marginalization for ethnic minority groups.

This general backdrop sets the scene and areas for debate, but we also need to look more closely at local service patterns, experiences and priorities with regard to ethnicity. What did our research show?

In exploring old Asian and Afro-Caribbean people's views about services and needs, we interviewed 71 people. A majority were sampled from individuals receiving a range of health and local authority services. Others were friends, neighbours or relatives of those sampled who were in receipt of services. Interviews were open-ended, but focused on people's perceptions of their current circumstances, – strengths as well as problems – in the context of their own biographies. We also discussed people's experiences with services. A second part of the study was to interview service providers (N = 51) from voluntary sector, health, social services and housing departments to explore their views about the needs of black and minority ethnic people and service provision.

'Yes, the community care plan should be translated. Then everyone will be able to not read it' (Service Provider). This wry yet perceptive comment is a good starting point for thinking about services' current perspectives on ethnicity, the typical debates and everyday dilemmas they face. It says something about services' awareness of the importance of ethnicity as an issue for services, yet not quite knowing how best to deal with it. It is also indicative of the services' problems of allocating scarce resources and determining priorities. It raises questions about service-centred documentation and about common service misunderstandings or assumptions that people from ethnic minorities are somehow always different from other people. It points to the many difficulties of the consultation process itself, including the muddles about language and communication, the nature of appropriate channels and giving voice to all sections of the community. In the following sections, we will discuss some of these points in so far as they relate to the views, experiences and stories of Asian and black people themselves.

Equitable Services

What did we learn about the provision of equitable services? Asian and black people generally do not appear at all concerned about this issue, though our findings suggest there is considerable evidence of service inequalities. Services generally do not have a central place in people's lives. Most of the Asian and black people we spoke to did not relate the priorities in their lives, their joys, problems and needs within a service context; many were keen to be and often were self-sufficient and independent. This, of course, is the pattern for most people, regardless of ethnicity. Most of the people who were receiving services were very satisfied with them. '[We're] happy with what we have' (Asian woman); '...We can't do nothing more, we're grateful to the Lord for what they're doing for us. Grateful for everything.' (African Caribbean woman); 'I'm happy with the home carer and all the services' (African Caribbean woman).

Most people did not know the name of the service they were receiving or which service a provider came from. Also, people generally failed to make any distinction between statutory and voluntary services. In addition, people were not primarily concerned about ethnicity in the context of services. So long as the service received was of good quality, reliable, available when needed and that user and provider could communicate reasonably well, then people generally were not so concerned about whether or not the service provider was white or Asian or black. 'Ethnicity' as an issue was not uppermost in people's minds at all. 'No complaints, she's an English home carer, it doesn't matter which.' (Asian woman); 'Most people don't need special Asian services, only the language and diet differences. The rest, I reckon it's the same for all.' (Asian woman); 'We don't expect services to offer Punjabi...don't see it as our right, but we really like it when there is an interpreter service there.' (Asian woman).

For some people gender was more important than ethnicity. For example, one Asian man, a widower, had refused a home carer because it would be inappropriate for him to have a woman calling at his house as he lived alone.

People were not normally concerned about equitable service care. What did concern Asian and black people were the day to day difficulties which a great many white people also face, the most common being housing, money and information. When people began to tell their stories about these problems, we discovered the kinds of difficulties they had found with services. Many of these, of course, do have a bearing on equitable service provision, however.

What are the issues about equitable care? We discuss these under five headings: access to services, service ethnocentrism, rationing, racism and disadvantages within disadvantaged groups.

Access to services involves knowledge of services. Many people did not know about the services available. One man said he knew more about services while he was working, but now retired and more in need of information he felt it was less available to him. Others said: 'it is difficult because we don't know what it is we don't know, yet need to know' (Asian man). 'I never ask no-one. It was only a matter of luck that [the service provider] passed through...'(Jamaican woman, about finding out about mobility allowance). People find it hard to easily find out what each service can offer, or which service is the 'right' one for a particular problem. Indeed, we know people's problems don't readily fit service categories, or neatly into health or social care. Barriers to access were also found where there was misinformation. Some people were confused when refused the help they expected with regard to aids and adaptations, not realizing the scope of the service.

Our previous work on knowledge and use of services has indicated there are common problems here: many white people also find services inaccessible, reasons for this including the lack of information (Atkin *et al.* 1989, Salutis Partnership 1992). However, Asian and black people face systematic barriers which further disadvantages them in terms of equality of care.

Language barriers, particularly at the point of first contact can have far reaching impact. Reception staff rarely spoke Asian languages and people were largely unaware of the interpreter services, which had been established relatively recently. Language barriers make common problems much more difficult. For example, waiting for aids or adaptations and uncertainties surrounding services' action is much more problematic for the person who is barred from making enquiries by not having a shared language. Language barriers reduce what little user-power there may be.

Misinformation or partial information about eligibility or service roles sometimes led to resentment on the part of providers who sometimes perceived clients as 'pushy' or demanding more than they were entitled to. In one family in which the father was very disabled, there were some avoidable difficulties regarding home care: 'Home help was a problem because we didn't know, weren't told what the job description was. So we had to keep asking and we asked for things she shouldn't do. Only it wasn't our fault – we just didn't know' (Daughter-in-law of a disabled Asian man). Being in touch with services did not necessarily mean that people's information or service needs were being met: '...they are unaware of other services which might be able to help, yet can't ask the auxiliary nurse because she doesn't speak Punjabi.' (field notes about an Asian man and his family); 'Language creates problems for us in getting benefits...the forms' (Asian woman). Statutory services tend to operate from bases which were far away from where people lived or were open at unsuitable times. Voluntary services, however, were located in the communities and much more accessible.

Another significant barrier to accessing services is the expectations that many Asian and black people have about what is appropriate for services to be doing for them. The person who sees a caring role for example, as part of the 'normal' pattern of things in family life, would be unlikely to look for service support which they may be entitled to and need. The term 'carer' is essentially a service-created category and more commonly used by white than Asian and black people (Eribo 1991).

Communication barriers were also in evidence. Communication is of course more than just language: it encompasses cultural, class and gender dimensions as well as verbal and non-verbal aspects. Good communication is vital for people when it comes to resolving life's problems and central to user-centred, needs-led services. Many people in our study reported communication difficulties which were restricting: 'I know nothing. I don't know what that examination was. I don't know what is wrong with my blood yet.' (African Caribbean woman, about her recent hospital visit). Strong accents and dialects mean that there are sometimes communication problems concerning people of African Caribbean origin. Service providers are sometimes unaware of any difficulties and services generally are less likely to address these problems because Asian language barriers have a higher profile.

Using family or friends to interpret may be difficult for the person and for others in a range of ways. Youngsters stay at home from school or friends are used to interpret sensitive matters. In the following example, there are other practical difficulties: 'My friends, who would interpret are usually at work at the times when I need help. You have to take someone with you...it's not so easy' (Asian man). However, we found that, in the main, people were extremely resourceful in coping with difficult situations: 'We communicate somehow...the nurses know what they're here for. Sometimes it's a Punjabi speaking nurse, that's good.' (Asian woman).

People generally seemed to be accepting and unquestioning of services. In some cases, people were afraid that the service might be reduced or withdrawn if they complained. In others, people seemed to feel they had no right or need to voice their views or opinions about services or their changing needs. 'I don't want to be a nuisance, seen as a trouble-maker, you settle for what takes place.' (African Caribbean woman).

Many people, particularly older people, recent immigrants and women may have had few opportunities to experience a system of services or, because of social roles, to be expected to engage with outside agencies. Service provider-user role relationships conventionally reflect a power differential which community care, in ideal terms, seeks to redress for all. In a partnership, both user and service provider have 'expertise' to share. Our data suggests that for ethnic minority groups, particularly women, this deferential role relationship is likely to remain a disadvantage and a real challenge to the development of user-centred services. Also, some Asian women may have had no need nor opportunity to learn to use the telephone, which may disadvantage them in terms of accessing services. A Muslim woman told us how she was unable to read the numbers on her phone which had been installed by social services.

Service ethnocentrism manifested itself in a variety of ways. First, services don't and can't meet all people's needs. However, where the services on offer are generally appropriate for the white majority only, such as sheltered housing residential accommodation and suitable respite care, then minority groups miss out. For example, an Asian woman left a residential home and rejoined her family because she was unhappy being the only Asian person there. An African Caribbean woman similarly left a day centre because she felt awkward being the only black person attending. There are few voluntary support groups for Asian and black carers.

Second, service categories and eligibility criteria can disadvantage Asian and black people. The concept of 'household', for example, which services use, does not readily fit the living and social patterns of some Asian families. An Asian man told us how he spends different periods of time living in turn with his grown up children. In another case the grandchild of an old Asian couple regularly slept across the road in their house; other women friends of the grandmother spent much of the day time with her in her home. Long-stay visits to families abroad may create difficulties about benefit payments and eligibility for later entitlements. Chronological age is a clear-cut marker for services, for example in terms of eligibility, client groups and provision. In some ethnic minority groups, there may be other markers of life stage, chronological age may not normally be a factor in determining peer groups or social groups. Locality, being near family, temples, mosques, churches or certain shops is an important feature of some black and Asian people's way of life, yet it is rarely reflected in the housing points system.

Third, cultural differences may be labelled, interpreted and responded to by services as a form of deviance. For example the importance of time-keeping, tone of voice and mannerisms may be misinterpreted by service providers.

Fourth, the tendency for services to hold on to unchallenged stereotypes and counter stereotypes about Asian and black people may mean that some people's needs may remain hidden, or that services are provided inequitably. Previous work has indicated that General Practitioners, with a key gate-keeping role, refer relatively fewer old Asian people than old white people to community nursing services (Badger et al. 1989). A further area can be seen in that services with 'special' provision for Asian and black people are not always successful. In our study the Asian meals service came under considerable criticism as well as praise by those who used it and some Asian people preferred English food. In addition, we found that for many people 'normal' expectations and cultural imperatives meant disadvantage when it came to services. For example, perspectives on health and illness often vary between cultural groups; response to being a patient may involve substantially differing behaviours and attitudes. In a service system where the 'norm' represents that of the white majority only, then there is scope for inequitable service provision.

Cultural requirements may mean that the front room needs to be kept as a formal place for visitors; this is not recognized by services as a 'legitimate' factor in housing considerations. For example, one service provider said: 'Most Asians come with a fixed idea of what they want – downstairs shower or extension etc. When we go we assess and see what the problem really is, e.g. they can't manage stairs so we offer a stair lift. But they find it hard to accept. Asians often want running water, we can't respond to culture on its own, we have to respond to physical need... We can't accept a need for, front room for visitors only, a cultural need for some.'

Service providers tend to have a different view about what Asian and black people need, and their service requirements. Perhaps this is also true for the way they view many white people's needs, but difficulties stem from the fact that even when these views are challenged, there is no systematic way for services to adequately find out about needs. Also, there are no readily available systems for feedback from Asian and black people; about their needs or about the value and effectiveness of services received. When people's concerns such as housing tend to remain low on services' priorities because services view their needs differently, then other problems may follow or existing ones be exacerbated.

Also, of course, the service intervention is likely to be less effective by failing to tackle the root causes; it may only be palliative and ultimately not cost-efficient. Interestingly, service providers in the voluntary sector were more likely to share the same view of priorities and problems as Asian and black people. Voluntary service providers were the only service providers to mention people's financial problems, based upon their experiences of dealing with these; many voluntary agencies offered valuable financial advice.

Rationing was also apparent throughout the research. Most people in our study were aware that resources and services these days are limited and that rationing needs to take place. They accepted that all their needs could not be met. Rationing takes many forms. Some is active, some passive; some comes from services, some is perhaps forced on individuals by circumstances. People cut down their own service because of an inability to pay. One black woman said that she could no longer afford the extra home care she felt she needed. The service used to be free. Another said that African Caribbean people should have greater benefits because they feel the cold more. A man had become unable to read his treasured books, but was afraid to have his eyes tested because he feared he would be unable to pay the fees. Ethnic minority groups continue to be economically disadvantaged in society; many of the current generation of older Asian and black people have reduced pension rights because they have not worked in Britain for long enough or their pension entitlements were built up abroad and are not transferable. It is likely therefore that poverty acts as a rationing device, despite the welfare state.

Self-rationing also occurs where people's needs remain hidden or unvoiced, as this comment from one woman suggests: 'I don't want to be a nuisance, seen as a troublemaker, you settle for whatever takes place.'

Where needs of a whole sections of the community are not translated into demand, large numbers of people are likely to remain disadvantaged. One person picked up on the political dimension. She felt that inability to speak English was used as a kind of rationing device: '...if you can speak English you can ask for more [services].' (Asian woman).

Services may be seen to ration support by restricting the services available. The lack of suitable housing for some older Asian and African Caribbean people therefore, represents a form of passive rationing. In one case a social worker decided not to refer a person for residential care because there would be no other person there from any ethnic minority group.

Racism was also evident. Very few people raised issues of racism as a 'problem', though clearly many have experienced racism in a variety of forms. Life-stories which included accounts of immigration, work in underpaid and often hazardous midland industries and difficulties in housing clearly indicated the extent of structural racism. Also, we were able to gain insights into the various ways racism permeates services in both overt and covert ways. Although our brief was to focus on people's perspectives and not on structured or other forms of racism, clearly it is a central part of the overall framework for exploring black and minority ethnic people and services. Racism sometimes appears as an issue with rather strange twists. One black woman told us how she did not want to complain about her white home carer, because she felt that it might make the supervisor think the home carer was being racist towards her. The problem was of a quite different nature.

Disadvantages emerge among the disadvantaged. Disadvantaged groups within ethnic minority groups seem generally to receive little systematic attention from services, although some service providers in our study were aware of this. We were able to identify groups who miss out on service support and yet who often face many material, health and social difficulties in their everyday lives. The local Bangladeshi community in the area of our study is relatively small and was seen to be receiving least service support and also to be marginalized within the ethnic minority community. The typical service response is often to equate small numbers with low priority. Older Asian women and lone Asian women were also found to have needs which were not being readily met by services. Some of the women had only recently arrived in this country to live, many spoke several languages but not English and some were encountering family problems. Their typical concerns were about isolation, family relationships and housing.

Equitable Services: Some Good News

The challenges to services in meeting the requirements of equitable service provision clearly are formidable. Our research, however, has shown that not all the news is bad. It is likely that similar examples of good practice and service initiatives may be identified in many towns and cities. We give here some examples of good news, as seen from the perspective of the people themselves. These examples may serve as pointers for future service initiatives.

Some 'good' services:

- A sheltered housing scheme, developed by ASRA for Asian older people was clearly meeting a service need with due sensitivity to ethnicity; a service which was unavailable in the statutory sector. Apart from providing choice on housing, it gave choice about a very difficult area for many – decision-making about breaking ties with traditional living patterns. Many of the residents, both men and women, felt that having found suitable accommodation, other problems, such as difficult family relationships, had lessened.

- An innovative service where a health advisory club was established at a church in response to the expressed information needs of the congregation. Another was an audiology unit's volunteer run clinics operating in the community.

- A service providing expertise which people needed was a sickle cell and thalassaemia project.

- Sign posting, attention to ways in which to help people find the 'right' service or information, was found in a combination of thoughtfully-developed roles, personal experiences and skills of post holders in the housing department and specialist sheltered housing.

- The local authority's interpreter and translator service, though unable to meet all the demand, was providing vital support for people across agencies. This was a service with due sensitivity to communication.

- Link workers were valued because they act as a bridge between people and services.

- Some voluntary sector organizations were meeting people's needs in a variety of ways: they were more user-centred, they tended to be located close to the people who needed them, provided a one-stop shop for all kinds of problems, were open at suitable times and were staffed by people who spoke relevant languages. They provided travelling 'expert' services on a regular basis, served as a base for a range of social activities, offered activities which reflected social groupings and interest groups rather than those bound by rigid eligibility criteria typical of their statutory run counterparts, e.g. age limits.

- A day centre was established as a result of a locally conducted survey of needs and run by those who used it. It is an example of the ways in which people can take charge of their own service needs. It also exemplifies the success of a 'bottom-up' service approach.

Needs-Led Assessment

In this section it is important to consider both community-wide and individual assessment of needs.

Needs: Community Consultation

We have already remarked on the comment made by a service provider about translating the community care plan; we touched on some of the difficulties and dilemmas which services face, including consultation. The main problems in terms of ethnicity and needs assessment seem to be those of inadequate existing information systems and inappropriate consultation programmes.

The new legal requirements for services to record ethnic group provide an opportunity for real progress, but it is likely that the base-line questions about the purpose of collecting such data and what they mean will remain unaddressed.

Consultation programmes are undergoing changes, but our study indicated that there are major problems here and that the whole consultation process requires fundamental rethinking. Consultation with any section of the community seems, at best, inadequate and fraught with difficulties; extensions of existing programmes, which are hardly effective for white communities, are unlikely to successfully tune in to the heart of ethnic minority groups. Community leaders may not represent all people's interests or views; Asian women, for example, may have little representation via religious or other leaders who are more often men.

Needs: Individual Assessment

Assessing any individual's needs is not an easy or straightforward task. Our research showed that in the case of Asian and black people, assessment may prove even more problematic both for them and for the assessor. The assessment is likely to be less valid than for a white person, for a range of reasons, thus leading to disadvantage for the person concerned.

We observed an English speaking service provider, with the aid of an interpreter, carry out an assessment of a Punjabi speaking woman's needs. This extract from our report raises many issues:

'The woman's English speaking daughter was unexpectedly at home also. The meeting began in a conversational way, with the assessor explaining his role and beginning to explore Mrs K's and her family's situation. Much emerged regarding the family's lifestyle and the difficulties arising for Mrs K due to her disabilities. The ambience was comfortable and relaxed and continued thus as Mrs K and her daughter enthusiastically and sympathetically helped the assessor in the onerous task of completing the assessment form.'

'I hate forms – they get in the way of proper conversation. But I have to do it – sorry – it takes for ever, goodness knows what they do with all this information.'

Questions were read out verbatim – the assessor seemed to feel at as much of a loss as Mrs K and her daughter regarding the complete irrelevance of some questions to the expected order of things in many Asian multi-generation households. For example – that it might not be usual for an older woman, recently arrived in England, however fit, to go out unaccompanied or unaided. Misunderstandings arose, for example:

'Are you able to wash yourself?'

'Yes, we do have a washing machine.'

When it came to fitting Mrs K and her family – not a particularly complex one – into the form's boxes, the assessor gave up.

However competent and committed the assessor and other professionals may be, this case draws attention to the danger that change becomes the goal in itself, and sight is lost of the tremendous opportunities for developing innovative approaches which do empower users, carers and workers too.'

There are other factors in relation to ethnicity which raise important concerns for assessment.

People may have different perspectives and values about health and illness from those of the dominant white culture. For example, an Asian family told us about the particular social stigma they felt concerning their son who has mental health problems and its meaning as a punishment on their family. 'Dependency' may be interpreted as a desirable and 'normal' part of the family life cycle for some minority ethnic groups, yet this conflicts with the service providers' 'norm' of striving to maintain independence. Also, Asian and Black 'carers' may not perceive their role as 'special' or one which is eligible for service support.

Unchallenged stereotypes and counter-stereotypes may distort service providers' interpretation of an Asian or black person's needs. We have already shown how, in our study, service providers had a different overall view of what Asian and black people's needs were.

Asian and black people may find it harder to feed back information about their service support and changing needs for many reasons. For example, communication difficulties, fear of withdrawal of service, or of being labelled as a troublemaker. Clearly without appropriate systems in place, ongoing effective care management will be limited.

The model of assessment predicated on the individual as client has many shortcomings, particularly for some people from minority ethnic groups. People seldom view their strengths and problems as separate from those of the social network of which they are a part. This also applies to the white majority, but is particularly true for Asian people.

Can Bradshaw's (1972) model of 'needs' be useful? We feel this model can help services focus on the ways ethnicity ought to be considered in relation to assessment and care management by raising important questions:

- Normative needs are those defined by experts on the basis of their professional assessments or on the scores of standardized scales, such as dependency measures. Are these definitions based on ethnocentric assumptions or ethnically insensitive scales or measures?

- Felt needs are equivalent to what people want. These are shaped by expectations, past experiences and knowledge about what services might be available. Are there differences between ethnic groups as to what the nature and level of felt needs may be?

- Expressed needs are equivalent to demand, action taken to express needs. What barriers are there for Asian and black people to express their perceived needs?

- Comparative need is the extent of similarity – or difference – between those receiving, and those not receiving the particular service in question. Overlap between the characteristics of users and non-users suggests there may be some people with unmet needs, and/or others who do not require or who should not be eligible for a service. How can we know services are equitable across all ethnic groups?

Ethnicity and Care Management: the Way Forward

Our research shows that achieving user-centred, needs-led services and equitable provision is a complex task. Many policy makers and planners recognize the centrality of ethnicity in the new arrangements for community care, but often have insufficient frameworks or information to fully address these issues satisfactorily. They are often hampered by ethnocentrism within the service traditions, structured racism, a legacy of policy neglect about ethnicity and a lack of training at all levels. 'Good practice' may be evident but services are often unaware of what it constitutes or where service strengths lie, thereby missing out on opportunities to build upon and extend appropriate services.

Current concerns of services about provision for people from black and minority ethnic groups tend to revolve around short and longer term practical questions, which in the main are service-centred. Services' concerns include the following: should the services be separate or common; should there be ethnic matching in terms of staffing or not; should there be adaption of existing services or development of new ones; which are the best ways to consult with all groups in the community; how can assessment processes be truly sensitive to ethnicity?

The concerns of service providers about ethnic minority groups are not the same as those of black and Asian people. Services need to establish guidelines for policy and practice, so that action can be taken to improve services within an effective framework which also encompasses monitoring and evaluation. What did our research suggest here?

Some guidelines for policy and planning emerged:

- All kinds and levels of services should be committed to equitable care.
- Ethnicity alongside age, class and gender should become part of mainstream planning and thinking.
- Every service provider should take responsibility for ethnic considerations; the first point of contact with services for an individual is absolutely crucial.
- Commonalities among people, not just differences, should inform services' thinking.
- Diversity within minority ethnic groups should be a major focus taking individual's own views concerning their ethnicity as key.
- Priority should be given to obtaining systematic feedback from Asian and black people who use services.
- Flexibility should inform all service planning.
- Recognition of 'good practice' within services and establishment of ways whereby others can learn from it.
- Priority should be given to obtaining relevant information about local communities and in consultation with all sections of them; people's lifestyles and expectations are very much influenced by local factors so there is likely to be considerable variation between

apparently similar ethnic minority groups living in different towns or cities.

- Development of interagency working, especially valuing the crucial role of voluntary sector agencies, should be a major concern.

'Successful' initiatives from people's points of view can help inform the best options for practical action. The following are some suggestions arising from our study for practical ideas for action:

- It is important to take people's views to do with the primacy of ethnicity regarding the nature of service offered.
- It is important to develop more sign posting functions in all services.
- It is important to ensure that every service provider can inform people about all services.
- It is important to make use of local networks; for example, a group of 'nosy' women in one small community provided valuable information to everyone locally – this might be tapped to help information exchange between services and possible users.
- It is important to give more resources to obviously useful service providers such as translators and interpreters.
- It is important to bring consultation to where people are and involve local people in setting up consultation strategies.
- It is important to make more regular opportunities for service providers to meet together across disciplines.
- It is important to develop an ethos of 'reflective practice'; each service provider every day and at all levels can use simple questions to reflect on whether they are paying sufficient attention to issues concerning ethnicity in their work.

Conclusion

This chapter is already a summary of some complex issues relating to care management and ethnicity. There are a few points to make in conclusion which we hope will highlight some key considerations and set the discussion and our research in context.

The first is that care management and ethnicity cannot be considered in isolation from wider historical and policy context. The whole of service care and care management is now firmly in the political arena. This means that ethnic minority groups continue to be disadvantaged in service provision. It is therefore imperative to take an explicitly anti-racist stance in current policy and practice within care management.

At the risk of stating the obvious, care management does not exist in a vacuum; any significant progress with regard to ethnic sensitivity and equitable provision can only happen when all agencies are involved across a broad front, at all levels and within agreed guidelines.

Despite evidence which shows considerable challenges to equitable, needs-led and user-centred services, there are many ways in which services can make progress in care management. Much can be done within current budget restraints and many things are being done well by services providers. Additionally, action in terms of service development needs to focus on the things which concern people most, notably in the vital areas of housing, information and finances.

Services need to be alert to the increasing diversity in lifestyles and patterns of living; the changing situations in which all people find themselves. Services need, above all, to be responsive and sensitive to change. The revolution that the new arrangements in community care signify present enormous opportunities for taking stock and service innovation. Resource restraints need not and should not restrain commitment, ideas and action.

References

Atkin, K., Cameron, E., Badger, F. and Evers, H., (1989) 'Asian elders' knowledge and future use of community social and health services.' *New Community* 15, 3, 376–382.

Badger, F., Cameron, E., Evers, H., Atkin, K. and Griffiths, R. (1989) 'Why don't GPs refer black disabled patients to district nursing?' *Health Trends* 21, 1, 31–2.

Blakemore, K. and Boneham, M. (1994) *Age, Race and Ethnicity: a Comparative Approach*. Buckingham: Open University Press.

Bradshaw, J. (1972) 'The concept of social need.' *New Society*, March 30, 640–3.

Cameron, E., Evers, H. and Badger, F. (1993) *You Get There in the End': Services for Old Black and Asian People in Wolverhampton*. Birmingham: Salutis Partnership.

Eribo, L. (1991) *The Support You Need: Information for Carers of Afro-Caribbean Elderly People*. London: Kings Fund Centre.

Salutis Partnership (1992) *Walsall Information Federation Research for the National Disability Information Federation*. Birmingham: Salutis Partnership.

CHAPTER 11

Developing Care Management

Judith Phillips and Bridget Penhale

Introduction

Although there has been much criticism of care management, it is clear that it is likely to be a core service to older people in the latter half of the 1990s and beyond. A second wave of care management development in both research and theory is sweeping America and at the same time more advanced approaches are being developed in practice. Whilst satisfactory evaluations of these initiatives are being constructed (Raiff and Shore 1993), social service departments in Britain are still grappling with the basic implementation of care management and are translating initial ideas into workable practice. The time is ripe therefore to develop research methods and set research agendas for the evaluation of care management into the next century. The concept (as outlined in Chapter 1) was embraced in this country on the basis of very little research evidence from the United States and we are vulnerable to repeating the mistakes that others have made if care management is not properly and continually reviewed and carefully evaluated.

This concluding chapter reviews the policy and practice developments within which care management is developing; it also considers the research questions highlighted in the preceeding chapters that need addressing if we are to have a clear understanding of how successful or otherwise the process is or may be in meeting its stated objectives and in particular the needs of older people.

Emerging Themes

From the preceeding chapters, a number of themes can be seen to be emerging in relation to the implementation of the reforms surrounding community care. Some of these were already in evidence at the time of implementation, in mid 1993; others have become more evident since that time as policy and practice in connection with work with adults and, in particular, community care, develop. Before moving to an examination of the research questions which might usefully be addressed in future, it is worth reviewing these themes in terms of the earlier chapters.

There would appear to be five basic themes which are discernible both in terms of the chapters contained within this volume and also rather more widely as the review of the literature has indicated in the first chapter. It is necessary to acknowledge from the outset that since the late 1980s there has been a burgeoning literature in this country concerning care management and assessment, following the American tradition.

The first and perhaps most notable theme is that developed within Chapter 8, by Davies, Baines and Chesterman. It is a good example of the work of the Personal Social Services Research Unit (PSSRU) at the University of Kent who have been involved in – and in many ways have been at the forefront of – developments in community care since before the Griffiths Report was published. This theme is very much oriented towards what might be considered the economic agenda, with an emphasis on finance, cost containment, value for money and quality. The expertise of the unit has developed within the sphere of the economic dimension of community care arrangements, as this chapter indicates. The Government explicitly chose to encourage both the philosophy and techniques developed by the PSSRU in a number of experimental projects around home care. Theirs was the model of social care which was referred to in the White Paper which preceded and to an extent justified the introduction of the subsequent legislation. What has been developed (Davies and Challis 1986; Davies et al. 1990) is a set of arguments and indeed a rationale for the tasks which must be completed if the provision of high quality home care is to be provided in a cost effective and efficient way; the chapter in this volume extends some of these arguments further.

The second theme is related very much to the types of material produced by the government and their agenda in implementing the arrangements: policy documents and guidance material. This is the 'how to do it' material, although as we have seen in Chapter 4, there has been a paucity of real guidance within such documents, many of which appear to be rather bland and inconsequential. The implementation of care management has focused on very specific aspects and practitioners are largely in a position of having to determine their own working practices and parameters with some assistance from the findings of researchers in this area. More recent documents commissioned by the Department of Health have attempted to deal with some of the issues around empowerment (Smale et al. 1993) and assisting in the incorporation of research findings into practice (Smale et al. 1994). What must be of central concern, however, is the mechanics of how this information derived from research is best disseminated, particularly to existing practitioners who may not have the benefit of planned, systematic up-dating or regular training opportunities.

The third theme revolves around a critical overview of the new arrangements for assessment and care management. As has already been acknowledged in Chapter 1, the original concepts of care management were developed and evolved in the United States. There are very real questions

for many people: academics, practitioners and researchers as to the transfer-
ability of these concepts from the US to this country and just how well the
ideas cross the water. Attempts to replicate or to continue some of the early
pilot projects have not necessarily been successful, particularly in the longer
term (the difference between a pilot project and widescale implementation
on a longer term more permanent basis, perhaps). Some of the outcomes of
specific research projects detailed within this volume, for example Chapter
2 by Petch and Chapter 5 by Bland, are suggestive of the potential difficulties
of implementing care management systems in the longer term with frail
elderly people, in particular those with cognitive impairments of the dementia type.

In addition, the needs of carers are raised in connection with such
systems in Chapter 4 by Futter and Penhale and Chapter 5 by Bland. There
has been much rhetoric with regard to the needs of carers within the policy
guidance; what has developed appears to be a somewhat tacit acknowledgement of the importance of carers without necessarily much evidence
of the practical support which the reforms were intended to bring about
(Department of Health 1992). This may perhaps not be surprising given the
lack of rights and entitlements for carers (to assessment or service provision)
contained within the original legislation which was enacted in 1990 and
implemented in April 1993. The right to an assessment is due to be rectified
with the passing of the Carer's Bill in Parliament in July 1995; this may not
rectify issues concerning entitlement to service provision, however.

The fourth theme surrounds issues of critical concern to consumers or
users of community care: choice, partnership, participation and empowerment. These are detailed within the original policy guidance documents
produced by government, without much indication originally for practitioners as to how these aims are to be achieved in practice. Chapter 4 by Futter
and Penhale touches on some of the issues that practitioners face with regard
to these issues within community care assessments with older people.
Chapter 6 picks up on similar issues of concern in relation to those elderly
people with dementia and questions how such notions as empowerment,
choice and advocacy might relate to this group of individuals. Chapter 10
by Cameron, Badger and Evers takes as it's locus of concern slightly wider
issues in connection with care management and ethnicity, but, within this
focus, critical concerns of choice, participation and empowerment of ethnic
minority elders are raised and addressed. And the chapter concerning care
planning and frail older women (Chapter 9 by Adams, Bornat and Prickett)
also concerns such issues as gender, identity and empowerment in relation
to life in a continuing care environment.

Chapter 7 by Barrett considers the use of language within the assessment
process. The chapter seeks greater understanding of how language is used
symbolically by older people. What is expressed explicitly may not be the
same as what is implied and different levels of meaning exist. The chapter
argues that some parts of verbal language may be used as a defence and a

coping mechanism by older people. When transferred to the arena of community care assessments this is of concern because what is being said may not be what is meant. Coded messages may be given throughout an assessment interview with implications for the outcome of the assessment and for user choice and empowerment.

The final themes surround a miscellany of issues: the place of multi-disciplinary assessment within wider care management systems (Caldock, Chapter 3), the position of carers of elderly people in relation to community care (Futter and Penhale, Chapter 4), care planning with frail elderly women resident on a continuing care ward (Adams, Bornat and Prickett, Chapter 9). All of these raise continuing important but differing issues to the patchwork which is community care as it appears to be developing. One of the crucial questions to be raised within the volume as a whole is the appropriateness (or otherwise) of community care for the population of elderly people in this country in the 1990s. The emphasis on the research agenda, which follows, may provide some illumination to this fundamental question.

Research Agendas

In mapping a research agenda four dimensions will be highlighted: client, practitioner, organization and attention to quality issues.

Client

Is care management meeting its original aims? The practice was designed to bring services together to sustain vulnerable people with complex needs, preferably in their home environments, yet there is still relatively little evidence to confirm that care management can fulfil this aim with all users. Much of our understanding of the operation of care management with older people comes from the initial demonstration projects which, as illustrated in Chapter 1, were extremely selective in their sample population. Although in practice care management has been applied widely, models of good practice remain localized and undisseminated, with no clear national picture of whom the process best serves (Hughes 1993).

There is also a dearth of research on how successful care management is or may be with certain client groups such as ethnic minorities with complex needs; older people with a learning disability and with captive clients and clients who may be in need of protection, often against their will. The notion of 'protective responsibility' as developed by Stevenson and Parsloe (1994) may be of assistance in this complex and sensitive area of work. Chapters 5 and 6 raised some important issues in this respect with particular reference to clients with dementia and calls for further attention to them.

As care management is applied to other groups, such as people with a physical handicap or learning disability, there are lessons which can be transferred. There is a need to pool research findings together and to compare in which situations and with which clients it is most successful. One of the least explored areas is the success of care management to resolve conflict between users. The consequences for people not receiving care management also needs to be examined beyond what we already know from the initial experiments. This is likely to be increasingly important with the introduction by resource conscious and constrained local authorities of ever more apparent rationing and gate-keeping strategies surrounding 'eligibility criteria for assessment and subsequent service provision. As the number of older clients of social services departments is likely to be greater than other adult client groups (by virtue of a larger overall population) it is crucial that attention is paid to the implementation of equal opportunities policies in the light of the development of eligibility criteria which may be discriminatory towards older people.

The practice content of care management also requires research scrutiny. Little evaluation has taken place on the timing and pace of interventions and on the relationship between specific intervention and desired client outcomes. The question of what the essential ingredients of care management are which are likely to lead to successful outcomes for clients is not yet answered.

Practitioner

Care managers need not be social workers and there are arguments suggesting that social workers may not be the most suitable practitioners in this respect within the process (Cohen and Fisher 1988). As care management has developed to date, it is primarily social workers who have taken on the role. Questions remain however over the ownership of care management: should it exclusively be a social work task? What other professionals possess the appropriate skills and knowledge to become care managers? What exactly is the value base of care management and what professional group can best and most effectively work within that particular value system? Is there any difference between care managers for frail older people and those who work with younger adults with mental health problems or learning difficulties?

Care management has also involved building new relationships with the voluntary and independent sectors and through new and different partnerships with clients and on inter-agency working within multi-disciplinary teams. Further research is needed to address the apparent tensions underlying these partnerships and how these may be impacting on the outcomes for individual clients.

As Petch outlines in Chapter 2 there is difficulty in reaching common criteria for care management – yet we do not know how this impacts on clients. Caldock in Chapter 3 raises the issue of how we move forward to the smooth functioning of multi-disciplinary care management – is this through training or through joint funding? Chapter 4, detailing the perspective of practitioner in relation to assessment processes (Futter and Penhale), outlines some of the current difficulties which practitioners face in terms of user involvement, choice and empowerment, particularly within the context of resource constraints, targeting and rationing. It is only through a thorough scrutiny of the outcomes of care management as it is currently operating that such questions and issues will be answered.

Similarly the insecurity and anxiety that some social workers express (Caldock 1993) requires monitoring, with research focusing on the motivations of workers in care management positions and the changing nature and perceptions of their role and functions over time.

A further question surrounds the precise role of the care manager – is it to promote and develop the independent sector; to co-ordinate service provision and monitor care packages of individuals, or become income collectors? How does this shift change the nature of social work practice? How far can or should independent providers shape the future of care management?

Organizational

Is care management more successful as an organizational and administrative system or does it truly benefit clients? Can the functions of advocacy and resource management be combined without too much tension and conflict for the practitioner? Is care management best operated by a team or through individuals are questions which remain only partially answered to date. Different service delivery models in terms of models of care management also need rigorous evaluation. For example, can the service brokerage model which until now has been largely developed for younger clients with learning disabilities (Brandon 1992) be successfully applied to older people?

Quality

The implementation and development of care management and the adoption of care management systems has taken place quickly with little emphasis on quality issues. Several research questions can be raised. For example, how rigorous are standards of practice and what is good care management practice? Is a quality level of care being provided as a result of the process and what changes are recorded in terms of client outcomes?

Research Methodology

In developing a methodology suitable to take these areas forward there are several key elements.

First, a longitudinal approach is required; to establish whether care management is better operated within a short term framework or whether it can be used on a long term basis requires a longitudinal study. Second, it is essential to involve users and carers fully in the design and implementation of the research. In addition, placing emphasis on user and carer perspectives on issues such as costs, efficiency, effectiveness and value for money is clearly crucial to the success of the endeavour.

The development of care management within the mixed economy of welfare is one of the major challenges to social services departments this century (if not the greatest challenge of the 1990s). Not only has it taken place within a restructuring of welfare but it has required a fundamental change in both policy and practice. For the majority of practitioners an attitudinal and cultural shift has been necessary, and for some is still underway. If we are to fully understand its impact on service users and their carers, those people for whom the reforms were intended to provide most support, then further refinement of the concept in practice and a greater emphasis on research from all perspectives is clearly required.

References

Brandon, D. (1992) 'Skills for service brokerage.' In S. Ramon (ed) *Care Management: Implications for Training*. Sheffield: ATSWE.

Caldock, K. (1993) 'A preliminary study of changes in assessment: examining the relationship between recent policy and practitioners.' *Knowledge, Opinions and Practice', Health and Social Care in the Community* 1, 3, 139–147.

Cohen, J. and Fisher, M. (1988) 'Recognition of mental health problems by doctors and social workers.' *Practice 1*, 3, 225–240.

Davies, B.P. and Challis, D. (1986) *Matching Resources to Needs in Community Care*. Canterbury: PSSRU, University of Kent at Canterbury.

Davies, B.P., Bebbington, A.C., Charnley, H. and Colleagues (1990) *Resources, Needs and Outcomes in Community-Based Care: a Comparative Study of the Production of Welfare in Ten Local Authorities in England and Wales*. Aldershot: PSSRU Studies, Avebury.

DOH (1992) *Foster/Laming letter: The Eight key tasks*. London: HMSO.

Hughes, B. (1993) 'A model for the comprehensive assessment of older people and their carers.' *British Journal of Social Work 23*, 4, 345–365.

Raiff, N.R. and Shore, B. (1993) *Advanced Case Management: New Strategies for the Nineties*. New York: Sage.

Smale, G., Tuson, G., with Biehal, N. and Marsh, P. (1993) *Empowerment, Assessment, Care Management and the Skilled Worker*. London: National Institute for Social Work, HMSO.

Smale, G., Tuson, G., Ahmad, B., Darvill, G., Domoney, L. and Sainsbury, E. (1994) *Negotiating Care in the Community*. London: NISW/HMSO.

Stevenson, O. and Parsloe, P. (1993) *Community Care and Empowerment*. London: Joseph Rowntree Foundation.

The Contributors

John Adams is a Senior Lecturer at Nene College, Peterborough.

Frances Badger is a Social Science Researcher with the Salutis Partnership, Birmingham and Honorary Research Fellow at the Department of Public Health Medicine, University of Birmingham.

Barry Baines is an Honorary Research Fellow at the Personal Social Services Research Unit, University of Kent, Canterbury.

David Barrett is Head of the Department of Professional Social Studies, University of Luton.

Rosemary Bland is Lecturer in Social Work at the University of Stirling. She is currently seconded to the Social Work Services Inspectorate of the Scottish Office.

Joanna Bornat is Senior Lecturer in the School of Health and Social Welfare, The Open University, Milton Keynes.

Kerry Caldock is Research Fellow at the Centre for Social Policy Research and Development, School of Sociology and Social Policy, University of Wales, Bangor.

Elaine Cameron is Lecturer in Sociology at the University of Wolverhampton, an Honorary Research Fellow at the Department of Public Health Medicine, University of Birmingham and a Social Science Researcher with the Salutis Partnership, Birmingham.

John Chesterman is Research Fellow at the Personal Social Services Research Unit, University of Kent, Canterbury.

Bleddyn Davies is Director of the Personal Social Services Research Unit, University of Kent, Canterbury.

Helen Evers is is a Social Science Researcher with the Salutis Partnership, Birmingham and Honorary Research Fellow at the Department of Public Health Medicine, University of Birmingham.

Christine Futter is a social worker specialising in work with older people for Norfolk Social Services Department.

Bridget Penhale is a lecturer in the Social Work Division at the University of Hull.

Alison Petch is Chair of the Nuffield Centre for Community Care, Glasgow University.

Judith Phillips is a Lecturer in Social Work and Gerontology in the Department of Applied Social Studies, University of Keele.

Mary Prickett is currently undertaking a period of professional training in nursing.

Mary Winner is currently working as a consultant on community care issues and is also involved in mediation work.

Subject Index

advocacy *x*, 71, 73, 76, 139
Afro-Caribbean, definition
    118
Ages and Lutz scores of
    users with/without
    dementia and
    comparators *62*
Alva *see* Central (Alva) pilot
    project
Alva pilot project 17
    indicators of and for care
        management–care
        managed cases *25*
    indicators of and for care
        management–non care
        managed cases *26*
American Long-Term Care
    Channelling Project 91
Asian
    and Afro-Caribbean old
        people's views about
        services and needs 120
    definition 118
    older women 126
assessment 95
    background 29-30
    individualized 43
    older people 73
    paperwork 9
    professional and user
        perspectives 31–3
    see also multi- disciplinary
        assessment; needs-led
        assessment
Attorney, power of 73
Audit Commission (1986) 60

Baltimore 95
Bangladeshi community 126
Barthel scores 104
biography 112
    instrumental use 105
Black, definition 118
Borders 14–5, 22

British Sheppey
    Community Care
    programme *xi*
British Society of
    Gerontology 99
budgets 49
bureaucracies, public 96
'Buxton Speech' (Fowler
    1985) 41

capitalism 84
care, informal 2
'Care in Action' (DHSS,
    1981) 41
care in the community *see*
    community care
care management
    definition 2
    introduction 1–3
care manager
    changing attitudes 6
    role 139
Care Programme Approach
    72
carers *x*, 76
    –sufferer relationship 65–6
    needs 136
    rights 54
    stress
        degree of 66
        at first and second
            interview *67*
case management 3, 48
    arrangements 87
    inputs 88, 89
    United States 48
case study 106-8
    Barbara Smith 106, 109
    Caroline White 108, 111, 112
    Laura Black 107–8, 110
    Norma Green 106–7, 110
Central (Alva) pilot project
    14-5, 23, 24
child abuse 30
choice 44, 46
client 9, 137–8
clinicians, behaviour 63
coded messages 79, 137
collaborative working *see*
    multi-disciplinary
    assessment
communication
    barriers 123
    difficulties 74–5, 130

Community Access Points
    (CAPs) 16
community care 54, 55, 99,
    120
    Act (1990) 5, 40, 46, 50
    reform *xi*, 34
    see also Kent (Thanet)
        Community Care
        Project *xi*
competition 35
conflict
    user-led participative
        services v.
        managerialist
        methods 32
    users 138
Conservative government,
    economic policies 41
consumerist perspective 44,
    71
continuing care ward 102–3
controlling site variations 92
costs 5, *98*
    home care 89, *97*
    rates of change *97*
counselling 9, 53
culture
    definition 118
    differences 124
    requirements 125
Cupar (Fife) pilot project
    14–15, 18
    evaluation 16
    main needs *19*
    referral pathway *17*

Darlington project 4
data collection analysis
    104–5
day care 68
    centre 128
de-institutionalization 41
dementia 60–9, 71–85
    sufferers, capacity to
        communicate 74–5
    sufferers *x*
Department of Health 1, 3,
    6, 34, 43
Department of Health and
    Social Security (DHSS) 7
disadvantaged minority 46

Duns pilot project 19
  first prioritized needs
    identified according to
    discipline 20
  identification of needs by
    assessors 22
  needs and care plans 21
  recording of needs 20

early intervention,
  importance 75
economic agenda 135
elderly, frail xi, 60–70, 102
Elderly Specialist Team
  (EST) 16
empathy 75
empirical analysis 91
empowerment 6
EPIC (Elderly People in
  Scotland) project 61
  carers 68
equal opportunities policy
  138
ethnic minorities,
  disadvantaged 126
ethnicity xi, 117–33
  care management, way
    forward 130–2
  definition 118
ethnocentrism 131
  service 124
exchange model 43

frail elderly xi, 60–70, 102

gate-keeping 71, 138
Gateshead study 61
General Practitioner 64–5, 77,
  124
geriatric care 102
Gilleard's Problem
  Checklist (1984) 65, 66
Gloucester Project (Open
  University) 3, 105, 113
Griffiths Report (1986) 8, 42,
  60
guardianship 74
guidance documentation,
  official 32

health
  advisory club 127

and illness, perspectives
  and values 129
home care 5
  carers 61
  costs 89, 97
  organizers 20
homestay duration
  (HOMEDUR) 90, 92
'household' concept 124

I/SWSG 18, 26
Implementing Caring for
  People (DOH) 7
independent sector 138
individualization 111–2
institutions, closure 2
integrated system 2
integration 109
interpreters 123
  and translator service,
    local authority 127

joint working see
  multi-disciplinary
  assessment

Kent
  (Thanet) Community
    Care Project xi, 3, 96
  University, Personal
    Social Services
    Research Unit
    (PSSRU) 1, 3, 4, 5, 135

language
  in assessment interviews x
  barriers 122
  as coping/defence
    mechanism 84
  social semiotics 81
  use 136
  verbal 136
    community care
      assessments 83–5
    misunderstanding
      79–85
Law Commission Report
  (1995) 73, 77
learning disability 2
life-history
  material xi
  story book 104, 106, 112
  work 105

link workers 127
literature 1–10, 5, 105–6
living, twelve activities
  (Roper, Logan and
  Tierney) 109
local authorities 7, 35
  interpreter and translator
    service 127
long-term care, efficiency xi,
  2, 87–100

market approach 45
Mead, G. 79, 81
medical models of care 30–1
Miami 95
misinformation 122
mixed economy, provision
  45
multi-disciplinary
  assessment 9, 28–37, 137
  and working ix

National Consumer Council
  (NCC) 75
National Health Service and
  Community Care Act
  (1990) 5, 40, 46, 60
  implementation 29
National Health Service
  Training Directorate,
  'Users and Carers: A
  Directory of Resources'
  72
National Institute for Social
  Work study (NISW) 62,
  68
need, objective analysis 46
needs
  carers 136
  community consultation
    128
  comparative 130
  expressed 130
  felt 130
  hierarchy (Maslow's) 110,
    112
  individual assessment 128
  model 130
  normative 130
  service led 19
needs-led assessment ix, 6,
  19, 29, 32–3, 40–56
  and ethnicity 128–30
nurses 20

nursing homes
    admission and caseload
        size for channelling
        sites 94
    logit prediction of
        transition to 93

occupational therapists 20
Open University Gloucester
    Project 3, 105, 113
overview, critical 135

partnership 48–9, 53, 71, 76
Personal Social Services
    Research Unit (PSSRU)
    (University of Kent) 1, 3,
    4, 5, 135
physically disabled 2
pilot projects 3, 14–27, 15
planning, care 95, 113
policy 60
    guidelines 131
    and practice development
        134–40
    service provision,
        organizational context
        119
political background 40
power-sharing 53
practice, themes 49
practitioner 138-9
Practitioner's Guide (DOH)
    46
'Priorities for Health and
    Social Services' (1976) 41
'problem solving' 110
production function 92
project management 3
'protective responsibility'
    138
psychogeriatricians 63
purchaser/provider split 9

quality 139

race, definition 118
racism 126, 131
rationing 125, 138
referral 17, 18
    late stage 68
    route 16
remembering, social context
    of 105

reminiscence 105
research
    agendas 137
    methodology 139
    programme 80–1
    project in continuing care
        wards 103–13
residential care 42
    see also nursing homes
resource
    implications 4
    management 139
resources 54
respite service 68

Scarcroft project (York) 4
Scotland
    EPIC 60
    pilot projects 14–27
Scottish Office Guidance 16
screening 15-8
'seamless service' 37
Seebohm report (1968) 30
self determination 71
self-rationing 126
Selfcare (D) rating scale for
    depression 104
service
    brokerage model 2, 139
    delivery models 72
    equitable 121
        good news 127-8
    and ethnicity 122, 123, 124
    provider-user role
        relationships 123
    providers xii
    requirements 125
sheltered housing scheme
    127
Sheppey and Tonbridge
    programmes 95–6
sign posting 127
social care
    models 30–1, 135
        entrepreneurship 2
    scheme users 62
social life 81
Social Service Select
    Committee (1990) 35
social services 2
Social Services Inspectorate
    54
social work 7–10

task-centred 8
social workers 9, 20, 138
    insecurity and anxiety 139
socio-economic background
    40
stereotypes 124, 130
stress, carers 66, 67
'substitute judgements' 75
symbolic interactionism 81

targeting 47–8, 53
Tayside 14–15, 22, 23
Thanet 61
theory 88

United Kingdom Central
    Council for Nursing
    Midwifery and Health
    Visiting', 'Standards
    for Records and
    Record Keeping' 113
United States 2–3, 48
user
    choice 71–85
    impairment, degree of 66
    participation 33

verbal, verbal language see
    language
verbal language see
    language, verbal
voluntary sector
    and independent sectors
        138
    organisations 127

Warner Report (1988) 42
welfare
    production of 4
    services, gatekeepers 71,
        138
well-being 103
White Papers
    (1989) 'Caring for People'
        43, 44, 48
    (1990) 'Caring for People'
        16, 29, 34, 36, 37, 47, 60
women, older
    Asian 126
    frail xi, 102

Author Index

Adair, J. 110, 112
Allen, I., Hogg, D. and Peace, S. 30
Baines, S., Saxby, P. and Ehlert, K. 112

Baldock, J. 32
Bernstein, B. 82
Beveridge, Sir W. 46
Biggs, S. 9
    and Wienstein, J. 7
Bradshaw, J. 47, 130

Caldock, K. 52
    and Nolan, M. 30
Callahan, J. 2
Cambridge, P. 7
Carcagno, G.J. et al 91, 92
Carter, G. and Steinberg, R. 2
Challis, D. 63
    et al 4, 5
Chesterman, J. 95
Coleman, P. 110
Connelly, N. and Goldberg, T. 8
Cook-Gumperz, J. and Gumperz, J. 82, 83, 84
Coupland, N.J. and Giles, H. 83
Cromwell, N. 45
Crossland, G. 41

Dalley, G. 33
Davies, B.P., Bebbington, A.C., Charnley, H. and Colleagues 89
Davies, M. 48
Devine, T. and Taylor, B. 43
Dowson, S. 34
Doyal, L. 46, 47

Elhert, K., Baines, S. and Saxby, P. 112
Ellis, K. 29, 30, 32, 33, 35, 48, 52

Fisher, M. 4, 36, 71
    and Marsh, P. 73
Fowler, N. 41

Giddens, A. 84
Giles, H. and Coupland, N.J. 83
Gilhooly, M.L.M. 67
Goldberg, T. and Connelly, N. 8
Gomm, R. et al 33
Gorbach, P., Levin, E. and Sinclair, I. 67
Grant, G. and Nolan, M. 31
Greene, V. 92, 99
Griffiths, Sir R. 5
Gumperz, J. and Cook-Gumperz, J. 82, 83, 84

Haight, B. 110
Halliday, M. 82
Hogg, D., Peace, S. and Allen, I. 30
Hollis, F. 8
Hoyes, L., Means, R. and LeGrand, J. 10
Hunter, D. 34
    and Wistow, G. 28
Huxley, P. 3, 7

Ilich, I. 52

Jack, R. 45

Kempshall, H. 47
Kenny, T. 33
Knapp, M. et al 6

LeGrand, J., Hoyes, L. and Means, R. 10
Levin, E., Sinclair, I. and Gorbach, P. 67
Lewis, J. 4
Lieberman, M.A. 30
Lipsky, M. 48
Lloyd, P. 32, 34
Logan, W.W., Tierney, A. and Roper, N. 109, 112

Mcknight, J. 44, 52
Marsh, P. and Fisher, M. 73
Maslow, A. 110, 112
Means, R.

LeGrand, J. and Hoyes, L. 10
    and Smith, R. 4, 7
Merriam, S.B. 110
Middleton, L. 36
Moxley, D. 2

Nolan, M. and Grant, G. 31

Parker, G. 67
Parsloe, P. and Stevenson, O. 44, 137
Parton, N. 8
Payne, M. 8
Peace, S., Allen, I. and Hogg, D. 30
Petch, A. et al 10
Phillips, J. 55
Phillipson, C. 45

Reed, J. and Robbins, I. 109
Reid, W. and Shyne, A. 8
Robbins, I. and Reed, J. 109
Roper, N., Logan, W.W. and Tierney, A. 109, 112

Saussure, F. 82
Saxby, P., Ehlert, K. and Baines, S. 112
Schorr, A.L. 52
Shyne, A. and Reid, W. 8
Sinclair, I. 45
    Gorbach, P. and Levin, E. 67
Smale, G. and Tuson, G. 43, 71
Smith, R.
    et al 9
    and Means, R. 4, 7
Stacey, M. 30
Steinberg, R. and Carter, G. 2
Stevenson, O. and Parsloe, P. 44, 137

Taylor, B. and Devine, T. 43
Tierney, A., Roper, N. and Logan, W.W. 109, 112
Tuson, G. and Smale, G. 43, 71

Wicks, M. M.P. 54
Wienstein, J. and Biggs, S. 7
Wistow, G. 34, 35
    and Hunter, D. 28

146